To C̸
FROM PHI
CHRISTMAS 1992

IMAGES OF FLIGHT

HOUNSLOW

IMAGES OF FLIGHT

A CANADIAN AVIATION PORTFOLIO

TEXT BY
WILLIAM J. WHEELER
FOREWORD BY ROBERT W. BRADFORD

Images of Flight
A Canadian Aviation Portfolio

Text Copyright © 1992 by William Wheeler
Paintings and Drawings Copyright © 1992 by the
Individual Artists

ISBN 0-88882-144-1

Publisher: Anthony Hawke
Editor: Dennis Mills
Designer: Gerard Williams
Composition: Robin Brass Studio
Printer: Book Art Inc.

Front Cover Illustration by Robert Bradford
Back Cover Illustration by Steve Snider

Publication was assisted by the Canada Council,
the Ontario Arts Council and the Ontario
Ministry of Culture and Communications.

Hounslow Press
A Division of Anthony R. Hawke Limited
124 Parkview Avenue
Willowdale, Ontario, Canada M2N 3Y5

Printed and bound in Hong Kong by
Book Art Inc., Toronto

To my wife, Pat,
who has been so patient and understanding

Curtiss Lark
William Wheeler

Contents

Curtiss-Reid Courier
Will Davies

Foreword

by Robert W. Bradford, oc

I believe that I speak for all aviation artists when I make the scandalous statement that we are very fortunate in being able to enjoy two loves at the same moment: aviation and art. Most of us who create our own little world of flight, on canvas or paper, became aware of our desire to draw and paint at a very early age — about the same time that we became aware of those remarkable machines that fly in the sky. That consciousness was nurtured into an undying romance with the aeroplane, a romance that, in many cases, later acquired another dimension, the element of history.

Since prehistoric times, mankind has produced individuals who have been compelled to record visually that which is socially, spiritually, or historically important to them. Evidence of this compulsion ranges from the mystical, stone-age, cave-art paintings at Altamira in northern Spain and at Lascaux in southern France to the space-age works of today. The artist has indeed become an important component in the preservation of our recorded human history. If we accept this conclusion, then we must ask the question, "Why is aviation history, itself, so important to us today, and what is the artist's role in preserving it?"

The answer is simply that the flying machine has shaped our modern affairs, in both peace and war, more than any other vehicle. Its social and economic impact on our lives defies measurement and yet the vast majority of our population, through no fault of their own, are unaware of what this remarkable invention has achieved for us. The "painted word" can help. It is true that World War II stimulated a proliferation of superb paintings depicting the aeroplane, and that war continues to do so. But the contribution of military aviation in times of peace, as well as civil aviation's place in our history, is largely unrecorded.

The enormous benefits provided for our country by the "flying canoes," the "flying dog sleds" and our world-famous airline development literally beg for the magic of the artist's brush. Yes, the aviation artist does have a significant place in the recording of Canada's aviation heritage. Add to this the beauty of the aeroplane and its environment and you have the formula for the energy that drives the aviation artist.

I was understandably impressed when Tony Hawke first spoke to me about his idea for this book. It was clear to me that such a book should be authored by a person who was both an accomplished aviation artist and who had demonstrated a life-long interest in the history of Canadian aviation. I had no hesitation in recommending William J. ("Bill") Wheeler who, for a quarter of a century, has been editor of the Canadian Aviation Historical Society's *Journal* and has also served a term as the Society's president. I am delighted that Tony Hawke accepted my recommendation.

William Wheeler's book, *Images of Flight,* will excite the artist and non-artist alike. At the same time it will help us to better understand the world in which we live.

I compliment Hounslow Press for making it possible for the reader to share these historical statements as seen through the eyes of the artists whose works are reproduced in this book. I am proud to be one of them.

Robert W. Bradford, OC

Robert Bradford (Bob to his friends) was born in Toronto on the twentieth anniversary of the Wright brothers' famous first flight at Kittyhawk. Educated in Toronto, his earliest connection with aviation art was with the Easy Built Model Aeroplane Company. He was 16 years old when he managed to save enough money for his first aeroplane ride — in a Gipsy Moth at Barker Field.

Two years later Bradford and his twin brother, Jim, both enlisted in the RCAF. His elementary flying training was on Tiger Moths at Prince Albert, Saskatchewan, from where he moved on to the Service Flying Training School at Vulcan, Alberta, to fly Avro Anson IIs. Sent overseas and awaiting posting to an Operational Training Unit, Bradford was temporarily assigned to flying navigational and bombing trainers on the Isle of Man. He was seriously injured in a bad-weather crash in the Cumbrian Mountains and spent several months in hospital. Back in the air, he flew Airspeed Oxfords on beam navigation training, and had satisfactorily completed his course when the war ended.

Returning to Canada, Bradford eventually joined A. V. Roe Canada's Avro Aircraft Division as a technical illustrator. His next move was to de Havilland Canada where he remained for 13 years, becoming chief illustrator in the Publications Department. In 1962, he created four paintings for Rolph Clark Stone, including the *Avro Jetliner* reproduced in this book. These works caught the attention of Ken Molson, the first curator of the National Aeronautical Collection, who commissioned the first of a further series of historical aviation pieces. In 1966, Robert Bradford joined the museum and a year later succeeded Molson as curator. He continued painting not only for the museum and private collectors but for Canada Post. From 1979 through 1982 he designed 16 aviation stamps. When he retired in 1989, he was the director of the National Aviation Museum. Since his retirement, Bradford has been able to devote all of his time to painting — not only aeroplanes but the rural scenes, which are another love.

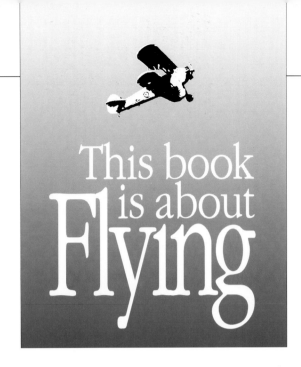

This book is about Flying

The 51 paintings in this book, by 15 Canadian artists who favour aeronautical subjects, depict the more historic aircraft flown by Canadians. Many of these aircraft are famous in their own right or are noteworthy for their association with celebrated pilots; still others typify an important type of aircraft or field of aerial endeavour. They represent all eras of powered, heavier-than-air flight and appear in order of the events depicted. Some of the paintings are well known, while others have never before been reproduced in colour.

Although aviation art is a relatively recent discipline and one that is recognized in no histories of art, it is heir to a proud tradition, with its obvious affinity to marine painting. An aeroplane, skirting mountains of cloud, with only a suggestion of the earth far below, shares the same romantic appeal as a sailing vessel heeling with the wind, ploughing through seas that extend to a distant horizon. The Dutch Baroque painters of the seventeenth century, the first great masters of the sea piece, were succeeded by the English a century later. It may be that the van de Veldes, Brookings and Spurlings have their modern counterparts in today's aviation artists. If J.M.W. Turner were still alive, the aeroplane against a turbulent sky might well be among his preferred subjects.

Robert W. Bradford

Robert Bradford, whose work comprises so much of this book, has been called the dean of Canadian aviation artists – with good reason. Bradford enjoys an international reputation and was recognized with an award for aircraft art from the American Aviation Historical Society in 1974. His appointment, in 1989, to membership in the Order of Canada honoured his dual accomplishments as an aviation artist and museologist. And so did the *Paul Tissandier Award* from the Fédération Aéronautique Internationale, which he received in 1981. The 25 Bradford paintings, which are reproduced here, were created over a span of more than 30 years. While there has been an abundance of work inspired by World War II air fighting – certainly the Spitfire has been a popular subject – only Robert Bradford has systematically re-created incidents from earlier periods of Canadian flying involving the more significant aircraft and personalities. Undoubtedly, his many years of association with the National Aviation Museum and his friendship with his predecessor as curator, the distinguished aviation historian, Ken Molson, have been factors contributing to the breadth of this remarkable coverage.

The Nostalgic Charm of Old Aircraft

The appeal of vintage aircraft, today, is comparable to that of the steam locomotive or the large sailing ship. But with so many restored historic aircraft still flying, there may not be the same poignancy. Nevertheless, aeroplanes of earlier eras have a firm hold on the public's imagination. This was proven by the unexpectedly large crowd, some 20,000, that recently turned out to witness the first flight of the Canadian Warplane Heritage's newly restored Avro Lancaster and its dedication to the memory of Andrew Mynarski, VC. Their Hawker Hurricane, the only one flying in North America, is equally popular.

On the civil side, when Doug Anderson's Stinson SR-9E Reliant (CF-OAZ*), Moe Servos's Beech 17 Staggerwing (CF-CCA), or George Neal's D.H. 87 Hornet Moth (CF-EEJ) appear at fly-ins, they are immediately surrounded by admiring crowds. Each of these sleekly gleaming beauties is over 50 years old. And there are many other flying "antiques," particularly in the USA. Still more are to be found, permanently grounded, in museums, where they can evoke both fascination – and sadness. Attempts to simulate, with props, an appropriate setting are seldom convincing. While there is a satisfaction in seeing the real thing, only the artist can create a window into the past.

* An explanation of aircraft registrations (such as CF-OAZ) can be found on page 126.

Changing Approaches in Aviation Art

The paintings by war artists Eric Aldwinckle and Charles Goldhamer (done almost half a century ago) and the more recent Spitfire by Don Anderson, also an official war artist, typify an approach rather different from that of those contemporary artists who produce "portraits" of aircraft. These war artists' concern was less with precise detail and more with capturing a telling overall impression. They would move from one squadron to another as their work was completed, choosing the units they wished to document. Much of what they did was created on the spot. They recorded all aspects of squadron activities from the dramatic to the mundane; one commanding officer accused them, not completely in jest, of being too partial to wrecked aircraft.

Aldwinckle was attached to 415 (Wellingtons), 430 (Photo 'Recce' – Reconnaissance – Mustangs) and 424 (Sunderlands) Squadrons, while Goldhamer was with 407 (Wellingtons) and Anderson with 404 (Coastal Command

Beaufighters), 6 Group (Halifaxes and Lancasters) and the Canadian Spitfire Wing. Working with operational units, they were able to paint subjects that can only be attempted today after careful research.

During World War I, artists also recorded the exploits of Canadians. Unfortunately no Canadian artists painted the airmen from Canada in the RFC and RNAS (both combined into the RAF) overseas. Frank (later Franz) Johnston created an impressive collection of watercolours and some oils of RFC/RAF training squadrons in Canada. Fred Varley did pen- and brush-line drawings of airmen for recruiting posters, and Arthur Lismer sketched the American units flying HS-2L flying boats out of Nova Scotia bases. Johnston, Lismer and Varley all became members of the original Group of Seven.

Painting the Sky

The challenges that face the aviation artist are very similar to those met by marine painters. There is the need to suggest vast distances convincingly and, in the case of the aviation artist, great height. To capture aircraft in their element, the artist needs a sound grasp of atmospheric perspective. Clouds, beyond the subject, must stay there, no matter how heavy and dramatic; they are still only vapour, softer and of less substance than any aircraft. And the ground must remain below – how far depends on altitude – suggested by the most subtle of value distinctions. Detail cannot be laboured, only hinted.

The Impressionists established for all time the importance to the artist of changing light. It must be believable, striking aircraft, clouds and the earth's surface consistently. Other factors may bear – cast shadow or reflected light – but credibility is foremost.

Similar drawing and compositional problems face both marine and aviation artists. The contours of a ship's hull require the same subtle modelling as the fuselage of an aircraft, with highlights used sparingly and placed precisely. Only a few edges should be sharply defined, while others are softened or lost. Biplanes, like sailing ships, possess rigging which must be drawn with care – and restraint. Clouds, in their infinite variety, are difficult to paint well, and their placement is crucial to the success of a composition; an indifferent background can detract from a well-rendered subject.

Minute observation of detail does not guarantee a successful painting – it must be subordinated to composition and overall harmony of treatment. Conventions – tricks – for rendering cloud, water, cityscapes, forests and other likely backgrounds can be useful; but used to excess, they are deadly. All of the units that make up any painting must hold together. When this has been achieved, only then can the artist indulge in a loving analysis of taught fabric, scuffed metal and gleaming perspex.

Self-criticism is important; no matter how successful the artist feels his work may be, he must not become too pleased with himself. In Robert Bradford's words: "When you are satisfied with your work, you are finished – in the truest sense of that word."

The Painting as a Whole

Famed aviation artist, Frank Wootton, whose work has inspired so many of his successors, has been compared with John Constable (his countryman of the previous century), who made innumerable cloud studies in order to avoid the traditional sunny-sky clichés of his predecessors. This sort of convincing freshness is very important to the aviation artist, who must also give equal consideration to whatever else may form his background, if only to decide how minimally each area should be handled.

Commenting on an original Wootton painting in the RAF Museum at Hendon, England, Tom Bjarnason, whose work appears in this book, observed that here was a beautiful painting – in which there happen to be aircraft. He was making the same important point: that a successful painting "hangs together," all parts combined in a convincing whole. Robert Bradford's *Rambler Solo* is just such a painting – the aircraft has not been superimposed on a background, it is part of it.

The Artists and Their Work

The paintings in this book vary greatly in style and media. Approaches range from a closely observed Realism to a vigorously brushed Impressionism – in oils, acrylics, casein, tempera, watercolours, inks, pastels, or in combinations of these. But all are consistent in their execution. Charles Goldhamer, for instance, in his painting *Takeoff* used watercolour (as did so many of his fellow war artists), applying broad, confident washes in the traditional English manner. Eric Aldwinckle, also a consummate watercolourist, chose to paint *Invasion Pattern* in oils, undoubtedly to make use of the surface textures that thickly applied oil paint makes possible.

"Very often I reflect on how fortunate I am to be able to combine two loves (flying and painting) in one singular expression – aviation art." This statement is by Robert Bradford, who was a wartime pilot in the RCAF before resuming his career as an artist. When he vividly re-creates moments in Canadian aviation history, the success he achieves is never by accident, but through meticulous preparation. His research is exhaustive; before beginning a work, he understands thoroughly the particular challenge of each subject. With many of his decisions made, his final painting, once begun, becomes a source of enjoyment and satisfaction. Now, he must make his aeroplanes "fly" – suggesting, in his words, "... the invisible fluid that supports them and adds a tantalizing element of mystery." He currently works in acrylics on stretched canvas, although many of his earlier pieces, some of which are reproduced on the following pages, have been done on illustration board, in designer colour.

Part of his preliminary work is a careful, small-scale, 'comprehensive' study to decide colour and compositional details. Bradford's studies are gems in themselves, quite different from his major pieces, and fortunately we are able to reproduce two – the Courier, p. 67, and the Mosquito, p. 95.

Tom Bjarnason works in pastels, but in a technique that owes little to tradition. His pigments, rubbed into the surface so thinly as to resemble transparent washes, have a luminosity that is well suited to reproduction. The *Dunnville Harvards, Junkers W. 34* and *Hornets in Readiness* paintings are handled in this manner, while his *CF-104 Starfighter,* done some years earlier, involves a very different technique – acrylic white combined with coloured inks. Viewers will see why Tom Bjarnason is an illustrator noted for highly individualistic work.

As a young war artist, Don Anderson proved himself to be among the finest draughtsmen of the group. Following the war, he resumed work as an illustrator and was soon ranked with the very best in the field, especially for his figure work, the most demanding form of illustration. Recently he has concentrated on an old specialty, painting aeroplanes.

The late Eric Aldwinckle produced beautifully direct watercolours as a war artist and many spontaneous drawings of airmen. In civil life, he was recognized for his work both in design and illustration; for a time, he worked as creative director for a major studio. His painting flair reflected his strength as a designer.

Huntley Brown is another established illustrator and painter with a distinctive style, identified by confident brushwork and bold, often unusual, colour. Working in acrylics or casein, he effectively blends opaque and transparent treatments.

Among his fellow illustrators, Will Davies is widely regarded as pre-eminent, and I am pleased to be able to include his *Early Newfoundland Aviation* in this book. Davies's painterly style, involving the thin application of oil colour, makes difficult passages appear easy. An accomplished draughtsman, he renders figures (the downfall of so many who paint aircraft) with the same deceptive ease. For this particular subject, little reliable colour data could be found – but this will not be apparent to the viewer. Red, the only certain colour, is used to advantage, with warm and cool greys subtly enlivening an almost monochrome painting.

A professional illustrator who is equally at home in oils or acrylics, Les Waller claims to enjoy working to a deadline. He is also a proficient glider pilot and the owner of a Schleicher Ka 6 sailplane. His love of soaring, simply of being aloft, is reflected in the enthusiasm he brings to painting aircraft and in the airiness and the drama of his compositions.

The tasks which the late Charles Goldhamer set himself, as a war artist, included the daunting one of documenting the work of plastic surgeons rebuilding the faces of badly burned airmen. The series of drawings which he produced are little known, yet they are among the most powerful art to come out of the war. He was an outstanding draughtsman and watercolourist. Following the war he became head of Canada's largest high school commercial art department; undoubtedly many graduates of Toronto's Central Tech benefitted from his knowledge and insights.

Don Connolly, a successful painter of aviation art, works in a traditional style, laying in broad areas and then refining. He develops his compositions through numerous preliminary pencil and colour studies, yet retains his freedom to revise and modify even in the final work. He describes himself as a "cut-and-paste" artist. A cherished ambition is to see a freer approach become acceptable in the painting of aeronautical subjects.

The lore of transport fascinates Bob Curry. He paints aircraft, trains and boats all in exacting detail, analyzing each surface and evolving a means of suggesting it. He researches his subjects thoroughly and paints with deliberation; a single work may take months to complete. *Guardian Angels* is a typical 'Curry'.

Graham Wragg's working style is the antithesis of Bob Curry's. A prolific painter of aeroplanes and occasionally of ships, Wragg works quickly yet with flair. He specializes in military aircraft from World War II to the present, often depicting particular aeroplanes for pilot patrons. He also undertakes commercial assignments such as book jackets, appreciating the selling job they must do. His *The Lynx and the Bear: Voodoo Intercept* suggests a lot of sky.

Steve Snider enjoys painting contemporary Canadian military aircraft, and his renderings capture especially well the power and appeal of the Canadian Forces' CF-18 Hornet. He works in a variety of media, and many of his commercial works – cover art – have been done in colour with linear accents. He, too, undertakes aircraft 'portraits' often creating a montage combining a pilot's likeness with views of his favourite aircraft.

Mike Martchenko is a Toronto art director and a very versatile illustrator whose entry into the field of aircraft painting is relatively recent. Previously, he had earned recognition in a totally different field of the graphic arts – illustrating children's books. His painting of

The Ruhr Express over Malton was recommended for inclusion by Ken Molson, who was closely connected with construction of the original aircraft.

Jim Bruce, a Montreal designer and illustrator, painted the *Avro Anson I* in 1971 as cover art for an issue of the CAHS *Journal*. Currently, Bruce's approach to painting aircraft is simpler, with a greater emphasis on atmospheric effect. He works with equal proficiency in watercolour or acrylics, and for many years, CAE Industries has featured his work in their promotional material.

Peter Mossman has spent a lifetime painting aeroplanes – aircraft profiles are a specialty – and he has an admitted enthusiasm for the Spitfire and for the F-86. His *Lynx on the Prowl* portrait is an example. There are many others who share his preferences. Mossman's fascination with gleaming metal is apparent.

My own works, which I have had the temerity to include – *Lt. Culley and the L. 53* (1963), *Hurricanes Attacking* (1965), and *The Heath Parasol* (1966) – were all executed in designer colour (gouache), a medium widely used in the '50s and '60s, but now largely superseded by acrylics. Looser, more impressionistic brushwork was also popular at the time.

Making Use of Reference

Successful aviation painting depends on good refererence. Sources may include photographs, models, sketches, technical drawings, video tapes, and even access to the actual aircraft. Photographs are used now to a greater degree than in the past. Few artists, today, actually set up before an aircraft and paint, as the war artists often did. It is now so much easier to obtain good pictorial reference.

And working on the spot, in the traditional 'bravura' manner, can be hazardous. Eric Aldwinckle told this writer of painting a wartime watercolour, seated behind a giant Short Sunderland flying boat under maintenance at a Coastal Command base in Scotland. He was totally absorbed in his work when, without warning, all of his materials were swept away in a blast of wind and noise. One of the four 1400 hp Hercules engines had just been fired up. The mechanics, their overhaul completed, were testing it.

Tom Bjarnason recalled a similar problem when he was chided about taking so many photos while on an illustrating assignment with the RCAF in Germany. Unable to convince his critic, he set up his easel in a hangar and began painting a C-130 Hercules – only to have it towed away in readiness for a flight.

Fortunately, the painting was almost finished.

How an artist makes use of his reference material is what separates the amateur from the professional. While the former may be capable of duplicating a photographic image with impressive fidelity, the latter is more concerned with interpretation and with being selective. The lens lays traps for the artist. Again in the words of Tom Bjarnason: knowing what to leave out (or correct) is the most difficult aspect of painting from a photograph. Not every rivet need be shown nor every access panel defined.

Canadian Aviation Historical Society

The reader will become aware of many references throughout this book to the Canadian Aviation Historical Society, particularly in the acknowledgment of paintings that have been prepared as covers for the Society's *Journal*. And much of my data, as well, have come from its pages. A number of CAHS members have assisted me with *Images of Flight*. Many of those whose help I am happy to acknowledge belong to the Society. In view of my lengthy and close involvement with the CAHS – and particularly the Society's magazine (almost 30 years) – I am sure that this will be understood.

On Selecting Contributors

There are a number of Canadian aviation artists who are not represented in this book. Those whose paintings do appear are the ones with whom I have become familiar, who have made their work available for use in the CAHS *Journal*. I consider it a privilege to have known all of them personally and to have become party to their views on the painting of aeroplanes. Unfortunately, Eric Aldwinckle and Charles Goldhamer are now deceased.

Space limitation was a further consideration. Several aircraft such as the de Havilland D.H. 82C Tiger Moth, or the Fleet 16B Finch – both World War II elementary trainers – might have been included, but were not. And it was agreed that this book should cover the full spectrum of powered, heavier-than-air flight in Canada. There would be no problem filling a sizeable book with paintings of contemporary military jets or of aircraft from World Wars I and II. Most aviation artists tend to specialize in these areas, probably because this is where public interest – and a market for prints – is seen to lie. Balancing them with civil types would be extremely difficult. To showcase the work of Canadian aviation artists as a whole would be a tempting and worthwhile project – but one that must await a future volume.

Acknowledgments

I would like to express my gratitude to the many people who have helped in the preparation of *Images of Flight*. First, there are the artists who so generously permitted me to reproduce their paintings: Don Anderson, Tom Bjarnason, Robert Bradford, Huntley Brown, Jim Bruce, Don Connolly, Bob Curry, Will Davies, Mike Martchenko, Peter Mossman, Les Waller and Graham Wragg.

I would also like to thank the many others who have encouraged and assisted, whether by making work available, by checking my text or by providing information: Doug Anderson; Dr David Baird; Arne Bauer of the Billy Bishop Heritage, Owen Sound, Ontario; William and Margaret Doherty of the Glenn Curtiss Museum, Hammondsport, New York; Mark Ducharme of the National Aviation Museum; Colin Fisher of de Havilland; Lynda and Robert Ewles of Amorak Publishing; George Fuller; John Griffin; Ken Hagarty; Hugh Halliday of the Canadian War Museum; Tony Hawke, my publisher who made it all possible; Fred Hotson; Bill Kent; Neil McArthur; David Metcalfe of Aviation Art Canada; Larry Milberry of Canav Books; Dennis Mills, my patient and very helpful editor; Ken Molson; Ms France Poulin of Pratt & Whitney Canada; Fred Shortt, curator of the National Aviation Museum; Chris Terry, director of the National Aviation Museum; Alan Wingate; and Mike Zafar of Paperboard Industries Corporation (amalgamated with Rolph Clark Stone).

William J. Wheeler

AN IMPRESSION LOOKING THROUGH
"D" FLIGHT HANGAR
ARMOUR HEIGHTS
S. OF S.F.

Canadian War Museum

Looking Through "D" Flight Hangar
Frank (later Franz) Johnston (1888–1949)

Year painted: 1917
Watercolour

List of
Entries and Paintings

"Casey" Baldwin and the *Red Wing*
Jim Bruce

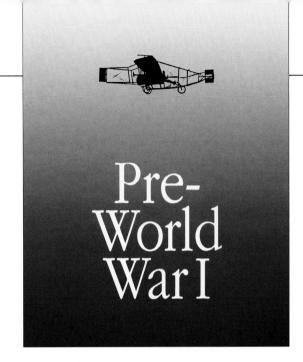

Pre-
World
War I

The fortuitous meeting in 1907 of two young graduates of the University of Toronto School of Engineering, Frederick W. ("Casey") Baldwin and John A. D. McCurdy, with famed inventor Dr Alexander Graham Bell resulted in the formation of the Aerial Experiment Association. They were visiting the Bell's summer home in Baddeck, N.S. Mrs Bell first proposed such a group – and generously provided funding from her private resources. Glenn H. Curtiss, an American builder of motorcycle engines, was invited to join the group because of his knowledge of powerplants; and it was in his factory at Hammondsport, N.Y., that all of the AEA machines were built. When Thomas Selfridge, a lieutenant in the US Army, joined the group, its international character was further emphasized.

While Canadians regard the *Silver Dart* as the most important of the aircraft built by the Aerial Experiment Association, Americans see this honour as belonging unquestionably to its predecessor, the *June Bug*. And their bias is understandable. The *June Bug*, with Glen Curtiss at the controls, won the Scientific American Trophy for the first officially observed North American flight of over one kilometer in one direction. To the members of the AEA, the *June Bug* was simply *Aerodrome No.3*.

On 12 March 1908, Baldwin took the *Red Wing,* the first powered aircraft built by the group, into the air to become the first British subject to fly a heavier-than-air machine. The *White Wing* followed it in May and then the *June Bug,* appropriately named by Dr Bell, in June. (The first two machines owed their names to the colour of their fabric.) Each had embodied lessons learned from its predecessors, especially relating to the control of an aircraft in flight. The *Silver Dart* capped the Association's efforts and incorporated all their knowledge of things aerodynamic.

The *June Bug* did all of its flying in a scant ten weeks, between 21 June and 31 August of 1908, at Hammondsport, and was never in Canada. But it has a strong Canadian significance. It was the aircraft in which J. A. D. McCurdy honed his flying skills. Canada's pioneer pilot had flown only once previously, in the *White Wing.* In the *June Bug,* built under the supervision of Glenn Curtiss, McCurdy made 20 of its 54 flights, including one of better than 10,500 feet. Only he and Curtiss ever flew this machine, which ended its days fitted with floats and renamed the *Loon.* Several attempts by McCurdy to lift it from the water were unsuccessful. Today, all that remains of the *June Bug* is a propeller in the Smithsonian Institution.

In the accompanying painting, created for William Doherty and his wife, Margaret, of the Glenn H. Curtiss Museum of Local History at Hammondsport, Robert Bradford has captured the *June Bug* in flight over Stony Brook Farm, the site of many of its triumphs.

33.0 cm x 45.0 cm (13" x 17 3/4")
William E. & Margaret Doherty,
Glenn Curtiss Museum, Hammondsport, N.Y.

The *June Bug* at Stony Brook Farm – 1908
Robert W. Bradford (1923 –   )

Year painted: 1990
Acrylic on canvas

When John A. D. McCurdy lifted the *Silver Dart* from the ice of Bras d'Or Lake near Baddeck, N.S., on 23 February 1909 and flew for half a mile, he was making history. For Canadians, the flight would prove to be the most memorable of the many achievements of the Aerial Experiment Association: it was the first powered flight by a Canadian in Canada, and, as the Royal Aeronautical Society later confirmed, the first such flight by a British subject in the Commonwealth.

The *Silver Dart* was a larger machine than its predecessor, the *June Bug,* with six feet, seven inches of additional wingspan. McCurdy had supervised its construction just as Curtiss had overseen the building of the *June Bug* and his associates saw it as his machine. McCurdy had flown the *Silver Dart* prior to the Baddeck demonstration. At Hammondsport, NY, he first air-tested it on 6 December 1908 and again on ten more occasions before Dr Bell had it crated and sent to Baddeck, N.S., in January 1909 for its Canadian debut.

Bradford's lovingly rendered acrylic is the product of considerable research. Over the course of the original *Silver Dart*'s brief life, a number of minor modifications were made and the artist has taken pains to establish just how the machine appeared at the time of its most historic flight. He states, "You will notice on the aircraft itself that between the main fore-and-aft members of the understructure and the cross-piece holding the forks for the nose wheel, there are two upright blocks. These were introduced to improve the take-off configuration." Just as the *Silver Dart* left the ground, Dr Bell is reported to have risen to his feet – the bearded figure standing bear-like in the bright red sleigh.

With its goals accomplished, the AEA was disolved, although Baldwin and McCurdy remained as a team. The *Silver Dart,* unfortunately, survived only until the summer. Aware that the US Army had seen military potential in the Wright brothers' machines, the two young men arranged to demonstrate the *Silver Dart* for the Canadian government at the Petawawa army camp in July. In spite of the soft, sandy terrain, the two aviators made four successful flights before seriously damaging the aircraft when a grassy hummock caught a wing on landing. The very similar *Baddeck I* (another AEA machine) also made four flights before it too came to grief. But mossbacks won the day; the senior officers present saw no military value in aircraft. The Canadian Army was not to become a pioneer in avia-tion. Today, only the *Silver Dart*'s Curtiss engine survives as a fascinating exhibit in the National Aviation Museum.

To commemorate the 50th anniversary of the *Silver Dart*'s first Canadian flight, Lionel McCaffrey, a member of the RCAF, persuaded that service to allow him to construct a replica. Eventually, two such machines were built, one to flying standards fitted with a modern 65 hp aircraft engine. This machine was air-tested at Trenton where it had been built and then shipped to Baddeck by air. W/C Paul Hartman, who had done all test flying of the new *Silver Dart*, successfully flew it from the ice of Bras d'Or Lake on 21 February 1959 and then took it up again two days later on the actual day of the anniversary. Conditions were not the best and Hartman's flying skills were severely tested. He succeeded in flying a reasonable distance, but a gust of wind resulted in a loss of control and one wing struck the ice. Part of the structure buckled, but the pilot was not hurt. Among those who witnessed the event was J. A. D. McCurdy, who personally congratulated and thanked Hartman. The replica now holds pride of place, the first exhibit to be seen by visitors entering the National Aviation Museum.

45.5 cm x 56.0 cm (18" x 22")
National Aviation Museum

The A.E.A. *Silver Dart* – 1909
Robert W. Bradford (1923–   )

Year painted: c.1965
Acrylic on canvas

Vought-Lillie Biplane

Montreal to Ottawa by Air: 1913

How better to publicize the launching of a new Montreal newspaper in October 1913 than by a feat of airmanship? So thought the editors of the brand new *Daily Mail* when they decided to have copies of their first edition delivered from Montreal to Ottawa by air. Sharing honours for the longest cross-country flight to be attempted in Canada to that time, and only the second to exceed 100 miles, the flight would be a challenge.

Selected for the adventure was a Vought-Lillie biplane with covered fuselage and slightly staggered wings, features that were ahead of their time. The aircraft had been designed for Max Lillie of Chicago by Chance M. Vought, later famous for the aircraft that would bear his name. Lillie built it and fitted it with a 50 hp Gnome rotary engine. To fly the aircraft, William Curtis ("Billy") Robinson, an American who had been trained by Lillie, had obtained his licence only the previous year.

Since the aircraft did not carry sufficient fuel for a non-stop trip, landings were scheduled at the towns of Choisy, Caledonia Springs and Leonard Station – all on the Canadian Pacific Railway line to Ottawa – where gasoline was available. Robinson left Snowdon Junction in Montreal in mid-morning, sent off by a crowd, his cargo of newspapers ceremoniously presented to him by the mayor. Instead of the scheduled three stops, five were required before he was to reach Ottawa. A leaking fuel line and a loose ignition wire had to be repaired at Lachine and Ste Anne de Bellevue respectively. These interruptions were turned to advantage by Robinson, who dropped off first editions on each occasion. When he finally arrived at his destination, Lansdowne Park, an unruly crowd surged onto the field, effectively preventing him from landing. Flying across the Rideau Canal, he was able to come down safely at Slattery's Field, and even there only an abrupt last-second manoeuvre avoided a horse that strayed into his path. Another crowd soon gathered; but the official greeting party, including the mayor of Ottawa, remained back at Lansdowne.

The 115-mile trip had required almost three hours of flying time; persistent head winds reduced the Vought-Lillie's ground speed to less than 40 miles per hour. From 2,500 feet, Robinson had observed fast passenger trains overtaking him on the line below, and Robert Bradford has captured one such instance through the low lying cloud and fog that obscured the ground for much of the trip.

As well as introducing the Montreal *Daily Mail* to a wider market, Robinson had flown the first commercial and the first inter-provincial cross-country flight in Canada.

24.0 cm x 28.0 cm (6^1/$_2$" x 11")
Collection of the artist

The First Montreal–Ottawa Flight – 1913
Robert W. Bradford (1923–)

Year painted: 1981
Acrylic on board

RFC Nieuport 12
William Wheeler

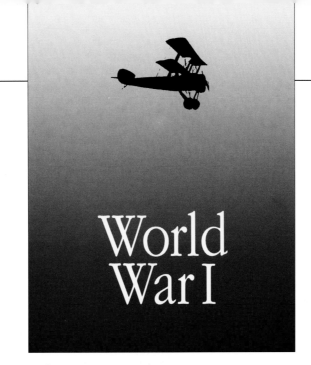

World War I

Burgess-Dunne Biplane

Canada's First Military Aeroplane

In September 1914, the Canadian government acquired the first and only aircraft that was ever to equip the short-lived Canadian Aviation Corps. The idea for such a service had originated with Ernest L. Janney, who felt that the First Canadian Expeditionary Force, due to sail for England on 2 October 1914, should include some form of air training component, and he approached federal Minister of Munitions and Defense, Sam Hughes, with his proposal.

Hughes's response was prompt and probably to Janney's surprise, since he was not a pilot and had never flown. He was appointed provisional commander of the new corps and allocated the sum of $5,000 to purchase a suitable aeroplane! This did not prove an easy assignment. He had no luck until he approached the Burgess Company of Marblehead, Massachusetts, who had on hand a single Dunne biplane, built the previous year. Their aircraft was powered with a 100 hp Curtiss OXX engine and was available, coincidentally, for $5,000. Conceived by the English designer, J. W. Dunne, the craft was unusual in that it was essentially a biplane flying wing, swept to provide stability, with an open nacelle to accommodate the pilot and a passenger. The only controls were a pair of levers that independently operated the ailerons on either side.

The machine was shipped by rail to East Alburg at the Canadian border on Lake Champlain where it was assembled. On 21 September, Janney, with company test pilot Clifford Webster doing the actual flying, took off and flew north following the Richelieu River. Against headwinds the 80-mile trip required 85 minutes and depleted their fuel. Reaching the St Lawrence, they alighted at the town of Sorel, Quebec – only to be arrested as German spies. Although a phone call to Ottawa set them once more on their way, they were able to fly for only 15 minutes before engine trouble forced them down. At Janney's insistance they pressed on. The engine seized and help had to be obtained from the manufacturer. They did not reach Quebec City until 1 October, scant hours before the *Athenia,* which was to take the Dunne overseas, was to sail. She was quickly stowed aboard. Webster returned home and Janney was joined by Lieutenant W. F. N. Sharpe, a trainee pilot, and Staff Sergeant H. A. Farr, a mechanic, making up the full complement of the Aviation Corps.

At their English destination, Bustard army camp on Salisbury Plain, the three found that the Dunne had been damaged, but they erected it anyway, although it could not be flown. Both Farr and Sharpe were transferred to the RFC; the latter unfortunately was killed in a training accident, becoming the first Canadian casualty of World War I. Janney shortly gave up his commission and returned to Canada, and the Aviation Corps was dissolved, an idea before its time. The Dunne was abandoned to the weather and souvenir hunters; when a search was made for it some time later, nothing remained.

The artist has chosen to depict the Burgess-Dunne in flight over the St Lawrence River. Although Bradford corresponded with Clifford Webster on the matter of the Canadian Ensign flying from the interplane struts, Webster could not recall whether the machine ever flew with them in place. The artist has taken what might be called "considered artistic licence" in showing them fluttering in the slipstream. The Ensigns are visible in black and white photos of the machine sitting in the water.

45.5 cm x 56.0 cm (18" x 22")
National Aviation Museum

Flight of the Burgess-Dunne – 1914
Robert W. Bradford (1923–)

Year painted: 1974
Acrylic on canvas

Curtiss "F" Boat

Equipping Canada's First Flying School

The first Curtiss aircraft to fly from water made use of a large single float, with the pilot seated above it or on the leading edge of the wing. The next logical step was to replace the float with a hull in which the pilot and possibly a passenger could be cleanly and comfortably enclosed. This was the genesis of the three Curtiss "F" Boats that were used by the Aviation School, which Curtiss Aeroplanes & Motors Limited established on Toronto Island near Hanlan's Point, somewhat south of the present airport.

In the spring of 1914, a Toronto businessman, W. A. Dean, purchased a two-place Curtiss "E" flying boat (direct predecessor of those illustrated) called the *Sunfish* and hired Theodore C. Macaulay as his pilot. Macaulay and the *Sunfish* immediately began to make news, first by carrying a Toronto reporter the 32 miles to Hamilton and back in May 1914, and then by flying another newsman over Toronto at 1,200 feet to take the first Canadian aerial photos.

A year later Canada was at war, and the Curtiss company of Hammondsport, New York, had established a Toronto factory, Curtiss Aeroplanes & Motors Limited. J. A. D. McCurdy, Canada's most successful exhibition flyer and the first British subject to fly in the Commonwealth, became the manager. In conjunction with their aircraft production, the firm set up a flying school with land-based flying from a field on the shore of Lake Ontario west of Toronto called Long Branch and the above-mentioned seaplane operation on the western edge of Toronto Harbour. Macaulay left the employ of Dean to take charge of the school (reporting directly to Curtiss) and instruct on the *Canada,* one of the school's complement of three flying boats. Guy ("Goggles") Gilpatric, who was later to become a well-known *Saturday Evening Post* author, flew the *Maple Leaf,* seen in the foreground of Robert Bradford's painting. The school's sheet-metal hangar, housing one of the boats, is in the background. The third Model F was the *Betty V,* piloted by Victor Vernon, and there were other part-time instructors as well.

Trainee pilots were given 200 minutes on the Curtiss boats and then a further 200 on the Curtiss JN-3 at Long Branch. Three and one-third hours of flying time was considered adequate instruction for a pilot. The cost was $400. In the first year, 67 pilots earned certificates, with 48 joining the Royal Naval Air Service and the remainder the Royal Flying Corps. The school operated again in 1916 but with instruction solely on land-based aircraft. Of a total of 385 students registered, 130 earned FAI (Federation Aeronautic International) certification. In its two years of operation, the school suffered no fatalities or even serious accidents. The Toronto Harbour facility was Canada's first flying school and first seaplane base.

45.5 cm x 56.0 cm (18" x 22")
National Aviation Museum

Curtiss "F" Flying Boat – 1914
Robert W. Bradford (1923–   )

Year painted: c.1963
Acrylic on canvas

Prior to the start of WWI the Curtiss Aeroplane & Motor Company of Hammondsport, New York, had been commissioned by a department store magnate to design and build a large flying boat capable of spanning the Atlantic. This aircraft, the Curtiss H-1 *America* had just been tested when the outbreak of war precluded the attempt. The big boat was shipped to England to become the progenitor of a long and successful line of such aircraft. After the Curtiss Company set up shop in Toronto with J. A. D. McCurdy as manager, they built a batch of JN-3 aircraft to fill British orders placed with the parent firm. Then, since the RFC urgently needed bombing aircraft, the new company undertook the design and production of a large, twin-engined bomber based upon the *America*.

The new machine, to be known as the Curtiss Canada, was begun in May of 1915 and completed ready for testing in September. Pioneer aviator Antony Jannus, the firm's test pilot, flew the big Curtiss from the Long Branch aerodrome with a British Air Ministry representative observing. The results were satisfactory, in spite of the emergency substitution of 90 hp engines where ones of 160 hp had been intended. The prototype was then dismantled and shipped to England for further trials. In Robert Bradford's painting, the Long Branch aerodrome site of the Curtiss Aviation School can be seen beneath the Canada's wide wings, spanning almost 76 feet.

In the meanwhile, the RFC placed an order for ten improved versions known as the C-1. But, by this time, the air war had intensified and it became essential that bombers be able to protect themselves from aerial attack. The three booms that carried the Canada's tailplane and the attendant maze of bracing wires made rear-firing armament impossible. Unable to outrun attacking enemy scouts, the Canada would be defenceless as a bomber. The painting confirms this.

Testing in England revealed that detail design and execution were unsatisfactory and that better propellers were needed. Since more suitable bombing machines were becoming available, a further order for 15 aircraft was cancelled and the Curtiss plant in Toronto was shortly taken over by Canadian Aeroplanes Limited for the production of JN-4(Can) trainers and F-5L Flying Boats.

Nevertheless, the building of the Curtiss Canada had resulted in many noteworthy firsts: it was the first twin-engined aeroplane designed and built in Canada, the first bomber designed here, the first Canadian design for a military aircraft, and the first Canadian design to go into production in Canada. Nothing remains today of the Curtiss Canada apart from records and photos. The eventual fate of the prototype Canada (and whatever use that may have been made of) the ten C-1s shipped overseas has not been recorded.

45.5 cm x 56.0 cm (18" x 22")
National Aviation Museum

Curtiss Canada at Long Branch – 1916
Robert W. Bradford (1923–   )

Year painted: 1967
Acrylic on canvas

The famous Curtiss Jenny in its several variations, probably the most familiar aircraft in North America during the early '20s, was undoubtedly the first aeroplane many people ever saw. It was the principal training aircraft in both Canada and the United States during World War I. Some 1,210 were built in Toronto by Canadian Aeroplanes Ltd., in a version that could be distinguished from its American counterpart mainly by the rounded and arguably more pleasing rudder shape. The Canadian machine had aileron interconnecting struts and it did not have the slightly downward canted engine, a feature of the numerous US-built JN-4Ds. These Canadian aircraft, improved versions of the JN-3, were universally known by the name "Canuck."

In 1917, the RFC (later the RAF) established 16 training squadrons (Nos. 78-93) in Southern Ontario: Leaside, Long Branch, and Armour Heights (all in or near Metropolitan Toronto); Beamsville in the Niagara Peninsula; Camp Borden, north of Toronto; and Camps Mohawk and Rathbun, near Deseronto. Later, in the winter of 1917-18, there were three schools in Texas as well.

Robert Bradford has painted a typical scene at one of these stations, the No.1 School of Aerial Fighting at Beamsville. Shown flying is a US-built JN-4A, and a comparison between it and the JN-4(Can) aircraft on the ground will make evident the differences between the two types. By later standards, the JN-4 family were ungainly and, with the 90 hp OX-5, marginally powered. However, they were stable and forgiving. The many hard landings, collisions with such things as trains and buildings, and outright crashes bound to be a part of such an extensive training program (and so often photographed), resulted in surprisingly few fatalities.

While the JN-4 was superseded as a trainer in Canada by the Avro 504K (its British contemporary), surplus examples sold readily on the postwar civilian market, with some 65 machines receiving Canadian civil registration. Hundreds more of the family, including many of Canadian manufacture, were active in the States. They were the principal equipment of the famous "barnstormers" who gave thousands their first aeroplane rides at country fairs. And they were also flown by the stuntmen who performed aerobatics at exhibitions or whenever there was the chance of a paying crowd.

Canucks were used for some early 'bush' flying, notably the transporting of prospectors to goldfields at Red Lake in Northern Ontario in 1926. The first Canadian airmail was flown in a JN-4(Can) as was the first crossing by air of the Canadian Rockies. An aerial survey carried out in Labrador in 1919 was among the first such ventures anywhere.

As the decade of the '20s came to an end, the JN-4s, which had been so common, gradually disappeared, succeeded by more compact and efficient aircraft. Happily, two have been preserved in Canada: a fine example in the National Aviation Museum and another in the Reynolds Aviation Museum at Wetaskiwin, Alberta. Several, including one Canuck, are flown by "antiquers" in the States.

45.5 cm x 56.0 cm (18" x 22")
National Aviation Museum

Curtiss JN-4s at Beamsville – **1917**
Robert W. Bradford (1923–)

Year painted: c.1966
Acrylic on canvas

Nieuport 17

Flown by W. A. Bishop, VC

One of the most successful and justly famous fighting planes of the First War was the Nieuport 17, flown by a such aces as Billy Bishop, Albert Ball, Georges Guynemer, Charles Nungesser and many more. The design originated with Auguste Delage of the Nieuport Company in France during the months immediately before the war and was developed continuously throughout the conflict.

Nieuports were readily identifiable by the contrast between upper and lower wing size, and by the distinctive wooden V-struts linking the narrow-chord lower wings with the much larger, slightly swept upper planes. This sesquiplane arrangement afforded the pilot a fine field of view. It also created a not-erroneous impression of fragility: in sustained dives the lower wing could twist, resulting in complete structural failure. Or, equally disastrous, fabric could peel from the leading edge of the upper wing. But within its limitations, the tiny Nieuport performed well, outclimbing most opposition, and with its spinning rotary engine was extremely agile.

In mid-1916, Nieuport 17s were made available to RFC units to make up a shortage in the supply of British-built aircraft. Some ten RFC and RNAS units found the nimble little scout to their liking. Among the most successful pilots was Canada's William Avery ("Billy") Bishop of 60 Squadron who amassed 47 of his 72 victories on Nieuports. In Robert Bradford's painting, which hangs in the Billy Bishop Heritage Museum at Owen Sound, Ontario, Bishop has caught an Albatros just as it left the ground. Bishop's initial burst from his Lewis gun, mounted above the wing, had missed. While Bishop corrected his aim, the German pilot, frantically trying to evade, collided with the trees bordering the field. This incident capped the solo dawn raid of 2 June 1918 for which Bishop was to receive the Victoria Cross. When more modern aircraft such as the S.E. 5Å became available, many of the RFC pilots had become so attached to their Nieuports that they were reluctant to exchange them.

An extremely faithful replica of the Nieuport 17 flown by Major Bishop, complete with its 110 hp LeRhone rotary engine, forms a part of the National Aeronautical Collection. This machine and the Sopwith Pup are regularly flown at airshows by carefully selected pilots. Unfortunately the Nieuport was involved in a crash, at the Abbotsford airshow in B.C. Damage was extensive and the aircraft is presently under reconstruction by museum staff.

90.0 cm x 105.5 cm (35 1/2" x 41 1/2")
Billy Bishop Heritage

Dawn Attack – 1917
Robert W. Bradford (1923–   )

Year painted: 1987
Acrylic on canvas

Sopwith Triplane
And the Famous Black Flight of Naval Ten

The triplane configuration which so readily distinguishes T. O. M. Sopwith's famous design was evolved in 1916 to provide a successor to the well-liked Pup, with improved visibility, manoeuverability and rate of climb. Delivered initially to the Royal Flying Corps, the Triplanes were given to the Royal Naval Air Service in exchange for their heavier and marginally faster Spads. (Spad was an acronym applied to aircraft produced by the Société Pour Aviation et ses Dérivés. These sturdy French fighters, also built in England, served with British and American as well as French air services.) In the hands of naval pilots, the Triplanes lived up to expectations, so much so that German counterparts were hastily constructed, notably the Fokker Dr.1 Triplane, flown by Werner Voss and Baron von Richthofen. While the Fokker design has proven popular with modern replica builders, because of its relative simplicity of construction, in many ways it was not as good a machine as the Sopwith that inspired it. The aerial war did not stand still, and it was decided that speed was as important as climbing ability. Although the Bentley-powered Camel replacements offered both, RNAS pilots were not happy about losing their "Tripehounds."

The Triplane illustrated, N 5487, was flown by Mel Alexander, a member of Raymond Collishaw's renowned "Black Flight" (B Flight) of No. 10 Squadron, Royal Naval Air Service, so called because the forward portions of their aircraft were painted black and the individual machines were named *Black Prince* (flown by Alexander), *Black Maria* (Collishaw), *Black Roger* (E. V. Reid), *Black Sheep* (G. E. Nash) and *Black Death* (J. E. Sharman). In just over four months, in mid-1917, this flight claimed 81 victories, 19 of them credited to Mel Alexander. One of these is depicted in Robert Bradford's acrylic painting, which was created for the Canadian Aviation Historical Society and presented to the National Aviation Museum on the occasion of his appointment as assistant curator. Bradford had been a CAHS director.

The Sopwith Triplane did not see service in Canada; but because of its strong Canadian connection, a replica of Raymond Collishaw's *Black Maria* has been constructed for the National Aviation Museum. Another has almost been completed, largely by the late Stan Green, for the Calgary Aerospace Museum.

67.5 cm x 57.5 cm (26½" x 22½")   **Sopwith Triplane N-5487 "Black Prince"** – 1917   Year painted: 1965
National Aviation Museum   Robert W. Bradford (1923–)   Acrylic on canvas

Sopwith Camel

The Most Successful Fighter of WW I

The Sopwith Camel was credited with bringing down more enemy aircraft than any other fighter of World War I – on either side. It has been described as the most manoeuverable production aircraft of all time. This agility, which undoubtedly contributed to its success, was due to its rotary engine, a radial arrangement of cylinders, to which the propeller was firmly bolted so that both spun around a stationary crankshaft, creating a powerful torque. Since most of the stability that had made its predecessor, the Pup, so popular with pilots had been eliminated in the Camel, the result was an aeroplane that had to be flown with caution and understanding. In the hands of a pilot able to exploit its quickness, it was the deadliest of opponents. But its unforgiving nature took a daunting toll among tyro pilots. It entered service in mid-1917 and was used in ever greater numbers until the Armistice. Well over 4,000 were built and they were credited with almost 1,300 victories. Many Canadians flew the Camel.

In the accompanying illustration, the Camel is a Bentley-powered naval version, and victory over its huge opponent has more to do with the tenacity of its young Canadian pilot than with manoeuverability. Eighteen-year-old Lt. Stuart D. Culley of the RNAS took off from a 30-foot deck, temporarily fitted to a lighter, towed behind a destroyer. At 30 knots, racing into the wind with the 150 hp engine spinning its fastest, the Camel became airborne as soon as the seamen holding each wingtip released them. Culley climbed steadily searching for a Zeppelin reported on its way to monitor a British naval force. He was at 18,000 feet when he spotted the giant cigar shape approaching. The airship was at least 1,000 feet higher.

Hanging on his prop, Culley struggled to claw his way just a few hundred feet closer. In the thin air, both pilot and craft were operating at their limits. And should they be spotted, they would be an easy target for the airship's gunners, who, like the rest of the crew, were on oxygen. With the Camel on the verge of stalling, Culley fired his twin Lewis guns, mounted above the wing, hoping they had not frozen. Their short burst was too much for the shuddering Camel fighting to hold its position. It stalled violently, literally tumbling from the sky. Culley regained control just in time to see flames bursting upward through the Zeppelin's envelope as the huge bags of hydrogen within ignited.

With the last of his fuel, Culley regained the fleet, setting down in the sea. He and his craft were both retrieved safely. Culley received the DSO for fighting the war's highest combat and bringing down the last Zeppelin, the L.53. His crewmen who risked their lives aboard the lighter were also decorated. Camel N6812 is now on exhibit in the Imperial War Museum in London, England. Another Camel can be seen in the Canadian War Museum in Ottawa.

Lt. Culley and the L. 53 – 1918
William Wheeler (1931–   )

Year painted: 1963
Gouache on board

43.0 cm x 28.0 cm (17" x 11")
Collection of the artist

Curtiss JN-4 making silent film
Tom Bjarnason

Flying
in the '20s

Martinsyde Raymor
The Aerial Challenge of the Atlantic

On 15 June 1919, John Alcock (pilot) and Arthur Whitten Brown (navigator) brought their twin-engined Vickers Vimy down in a bog at Clifden, Ireland, after a 16-hour and 28-minute flight from Lester's Field, near St John's, Newfoundland. They had just won a dangerous and demanding contest, against determined competition. Theirs was a prize first offered prior to World War I, a sum of £10,000 to be given by the London *Daily Mail* to the crew who made the first non-stop trans-Atlantic crossing by air.

Among the unsuccessful contenders was the Martinsyde *Raymor* flown by F. P. Raynham with Commander C. F. W. Morgan RN as his navigator. It made two attempts to become airborne from the shore of Quidi Vidi Lake but on both occasions was unable to leave the ground. Each time, a combination of overloading and rough terrain caused its undercarriage to give way. The *Raymor* was derived from the Martinsyde Buzzard fighter that appeared late in World War I. The *Raymor* is shown in the two uppermost views in the montage prepared by Will Davies as a cover for the CAHS *Journal*. At the bottom is a Westland Limousine III used by Sidney Cotton in Newfoundland in the early '20s. The painting epitomizes the artist's distinctive style and the draughtsmanship that has earned him recognition as one of the very best in his field.

Just hours before the *Raymor*'s unsuccessful attempt to take off, Harry Hawker (pilot) and Kenneth Mackenzie-Grieve (navigator) had gotten away successfully in their Sopwith *Atlantic* only to be forced down in mid-Atlantic with an overheated engine. Fortunately a nearby Danish merchantman rescued them from very heavy seas. The fourth contender was a Handley Page V/1500 four-engined World War I bomber designed to raid Berlin from bases in England. But, by the time it was ready for flight, Alcock and Brown had already taken the prize, and the giant bomber flew instead to the United States (but not without mishap) to be demonstrated. Its size impressed many.

There were two other successful trans-Atlantic flights in 1919 but neither qualified for the *Daily Mail* prize. In May, three US Navy Curtiss NC flying boats had stopped at Trepassey Bay, Newfoundland, before leaving for the Azores. There would have been four, but the NC-2 was badly damaged in a fire prior to the flight. Of the three, only one 'Nancy' arrived by air. The NC-1 came down at sea where one of the picket line of destroyers stationed along their route rescued the crew. The NC-3 also came down at sea; although their boat was badly damaged, the crew succeeded, by drfting and judicious taxiing, in reaching one of the Azore islands. Only the NC-4 was able to fly on to Portugal, then Spain and finally to Plymouth, England, to complete the flight. Since the Azores landing negated the non-stop requirement, the Nancy was not eligible for the prize.

The third successful flight was made from east to west and was not by a heavier-than-air machine. The British dirigible R-34, 640 feet long and with five 250 hp engines, left East Fortune in Scotland on 2 July and arrived over Mineola in New York State four days later. With favourable winds, it returned to England in only three days – a matter-of-fact accomplishment, without great fanfare. All of this was eight years before Charles Lindbergh's solo New York–Paris flight capped the next great surge in trans-Atlantic flying.

40.5 cm x 43.0 cm (16" x 17")
Whereabouts unknown

Early Aviation in Newfoundland – 1919
Will Davies (1924–   )

Year painted: 1988
Oil on board

Curtiss HS-2L

Canada's First 'Bush Plane'

Under the stimulus of war, the improvements in aircraft performance between 1914 and 1918 were immense, and the potential for adapting suitable military machines to post-war civil use was obvious. Nowhere was this more apparent than in Canada, where distances are so vast. And one of the types most readily available here was the Curtiss HS-2L maritime patrol bomber.

When the US Navy left their base at Halifax, N.S., following the Armistice, they turned their complement of 12 HS-2Ls over to the Canadian government. Two of these were acquired by the St Maurice Forestry Protective Association of Quebec (soon to become Laurentide Air Service) for fire patrol and related duties. The first, collected by Stuart Graham on 5 June 1919, eventually bore Canadian civil registration G-CAAC. In September 1922, she fatefully dug a wingtip into the water during an attempted takeoff. In 1968 her remains, well preserved in the silt of the lake bottom, were salvaged and removed to the National Aviation Museum where they now form a fascinating display. But G-CAAC, also known as *La Vigilance*, was to gain new life; reconstructed by the staff of the museum with some fittings from the original aircraft and parts from two others, it has become the only Curtiss HS-2L in existence.

The remaining ten USN HS-2Ls were turned over to the fledgling Canadian Air Board and, with 20 more, were placed in service all across Canada. The other principal user of the big boats was the Ontario Provincial Air Service which operated a fleet of 21 (not all at any one time) from 1924 until 1932, when the last was retired. They inspired a love/hate relationship with their crews including many whose names were to become well known in Canadian aviation. Although they were ungainly aircraft for bush operation – with a span of 73 feet – and carried only five people or a minimal cargo, they performed adequately until more-efficient replacements became available. Each fall they were taken from the water to allow their water-logged wooden hulls to dry out. Their big 360 hp Liberty engines were overhauled and airframes reconditioned, ready for spring breakup and the next season's operations.

When the Air Board, which controlled all flying in Canada, decided that a trans-Canada flight in the fall of 1920 would foster public confidence in aviation, one of their HS-2Ls, bearing government registration G-CYAG, flew most of the first leg. It replaced the machine that began the flight, the Fairey IIIC(mod) seaplane (G-CYCF) *Transatlantic* (originally intended for a trans-Atlantic attempt) which had broken down – fortunately not in mid-Atlantic! Col. Robert Leckie (later Air Marshal) flew G-CYAG from Saint John, N.B. to Rivière-du-Loup. His flying skill was amply proven when he had to bring his boat down in pitch darkness amid driving rain. Artist Robert Bradford has relied upon the meagre light of a lantern mounted on a buoy to illuminate this tense moment.

45.5 cm x 56.0 cm (18" x 22")
National Aviation Museum

Curtiss HS-2L – 1920
Robert W. Bradford (1923–)

Year painted: c.1966
Acrylic on board

de Havilland D.H. 9A

A Versatile Aeroplane

The de Havilland D.H. 9A was developed from the less-than-popular D.H. 9. The 9A owed its success to the marriage of its predecessor's airframe, substantially modified, with the American-designed and -built 400 hp Liberty engine. Known as the "Nine Ack," it performed its role of day bomber effectively and with minimal losses, being able to maintain altitude and, flying in formation, to fight off attacking scouts. Active for only the last few months of World War I, it was to remain in peacetime RAF operation for many years after, and the design subsequently became the basis for the Westland Wapiti and Wallace types. Under the American designation DH-4, it was built in the US postwar for the US Army

Air Service and used to fly the airmail. Most US variants had more in common with the 9A than with their namesake, the D.H. 4.

The Imperial Gift, which provided Canada's postwar air force with its initial equipment, included 12 D.H. 9As and an equal number of slightly smaller D.H. 4s. Four of the former were chosen to complete the western half of the trans-Canada flight of 1920, from Winnipeg on. The last leg, from Calgary west, was to be flown by G-CYBF, piloted by Captain G. A. Thompson and accompanied by Lt/Col Arthur Tylee, commanding officer of the then Canadian Air Force. They took off at mid-day on 13 October, late in the year for mountain flying, making their way safely up the Bow

Valley to Banff and on through the Kicking Horse Pass to Field and then to Golden. A snowstorm stranded them at Revelstoke, where they had stopped to refuel. On the 15th they were again in the air and got as far as Merritt, only to be trapped there by weather until the 17th. The trip was completed skimming above the Fraser River, with canyon walls on either side and a lowering ceiling overhead.

Robert Bradford has chosen to paint 'BF (G-CYBF) flying through low cloud against the massive, snow-shrouded walls of a canyon in the Selkirk Mountains, well illustrating the daunting nature of the flight. No examples of the D.H. 4/9/9A series exist in Canada.

45.5 cm x 56.0 cm (18" x 22")
National Aviation Museum

D.H. 9A Trans Canada Flight – 1920
Robert W. Bradford (1923–)

Year painted: c.1964
Acrylic on canvas

A Very Famous Trainer

Few Canadian fighter pilots of the First Great War did not have instructional time on the Avro 504, especially if they were to fly the rotary-engined fighters that were unique to the period – the Nieuports and Sopwiths. With both the engine and prop spinning as one, there was considerable torque to counteract. Understood, it could be used to advantage, but for the novice it was an ever present hazard, especially in the notoriously unstable Camel. The 504 provided a gentle introduction to these characteristics, which could come as a shock – occasionally fatal – to pilots fresh from the stable JN-4 with its convential in-line engine.

The design was conceived by Alliot Verdon Roe in 1913. As the best-performing aircraft available in the early months of the war, 504s carried out bombing raids into Germany and even did duty as night fighters. They were soon succeeded in these roles by more powerful aircraft – to take up a calling as trainers where they excelled. The widely used Gosport method of flight instruction (in which pilots learned why aircraft flew and how they responded to their controls) evolved around the 504K.

Following the completion of JN-4(Can) production, Canadian Aeroplanes Limited had accepted a contract to build a version of the 504. Only a couple were completed prior to the Armistice and just one was delivered to the RAF in Canada. However, 62 Avro trainers comprising over half of the 1919 Imperial Gift were turned over to the Canadian Air Board by the British government and remained in service with the RCAF until 1928. Smaller machines such as the de Havilland D.H. 60 Moth, Avro Avian and Curtiss-Reid Rambler succeeded them. They were the sole primary training aircraft of the CAF and, after 1924, of the RCAF. In 1925, their wartime khaki-green colour scheme with government registration applied on white panels gave way to the golden yellow, which has become traditional for training aircraft. Robert Bradford has de-picted a typically busy day at Camp Borden, where much of the training on the 504 was carried out.

Other variants of the 504, notably the 504N with the A.S. Lynx radial engine, and the 552A with the Wolsley Viper (British-built Hispano-Suiza), were used on forestry patrol. Small numbers of the "Lynx Avro" and the "Avro Viper" as they were respectively called in the RCAF were built by Canadian Vickers. They operated on wheels or with beautifully finished, single mahogany floats. Fewer than a dozen 504s or their derivatives found their way into civilian operation.

The National Aviation Museum possesses three 504Ks, two rebuilt from original machines and one complete reconstruction, all readied in time for Canada's 1967 Centennial-year celebrations. One of these is on long-term loan to the Western Canada Aviation Museum in Winnipeg.

45.5 cm x 56.0 cm (18" x 22")
National Aviation Museum

Avro 504K – 1924
Robert W. Bradford (1923–)

Year painted: 1963–65
Acrylic on canvas

Douglas MO-2BS

First Across Canada on Floats

Outstanding individual achievement in Canadian aviation has been recognized annually since 1927 by the presentation of the McKee Trans-Canada Trophy, an award donated by the man whose name it bears. James Dalzell McKee was not a Canadian, but he contributed significantly to aviation in this country. Unfortunately, he did not live to see the initial presentation of his trophy to H. A. "Doc" Oaks for his pioneer work in bush flying with Western Canada Airways.

Captain McKee, a reserve officer in the United States Army Air Service, came from a wealthy family and thus had the means to purchase a Douglas O-2B military observation machine, powered with a 400 hp Liberty engine. He felt this aircraft would be suitable for exploring the Canadian North. An 'M' was added to the designation of the Douglas to indicate that it had been modified, and an 'S'

when it was fitted with floats – hence the designation MO-2BS. Accompanied by an American naval officer, McKee arrived in Sudbury in August of 1926 and made ready for a flight into the James Bay region, only to find that his aircraft would not lift a full load of fuel and supplies off fresh water. (It had performed adequately from salt water). The Canadian Vickers Company of Montreal, at the Douglas firm's suggestion, shortened the rear float-struts slightly, and this seemed to solve the problem. However, the California-based manufacturer requested that the machine be returned to them for thorough testing.

McKee decided to fly his Douglas across Canada, a feat never before attempted by a single seaplane and crew. Accompanying him was Squadron Leader A. Earl Godfrey, who took temporary leave of his posting as superintendent of Civil Government Air Op-

erations with the RCAF. The flight was accomplished successfully, although not without incident, between September 11 and 19, 1926. Strong headwinds and heavy rain in Ontario were the severest challenges.

McKee returned to Canada only to be drowned in the glassy water-crash of a Vickers Vedette, which he had purchased to accompany the Douglas on his expedition into northern Canada. Before his death, he had obtained the trophy that was to bear his name and arranged for its annual presentation. S/L (later Air Vice-Marshal) Godfrey himself was to be awarded the trophy somewhat belatedly in 1977.

In Les Waller's lively acrylic painting, the olive-drab Douglas – it bore no markings whatever – is shown negotiating a British Columbia river valley, on the final stage of its trip to the west coast

27.3 cm x 26.0 cm (10 ¾" x 10 ¼")
Collection of the artist

Douglas MO-2BS – 1926
Les Waller (1931–   )

Year painted: 1990
Gouache on board

Armstrong Whitworth Siskin
Canada's Pre-War First-Line Fighter

About the only aircraft of a warlike nature flown by the pre-war RCAF – apart from 25 ancient Wapitis and 16 Atlases used for army co-operation – were a dozen Armstrong Whitworth Siskin fighters. Although few in number, Canadians fondly remember them for the aerobatic displays that they performed in the early '30s. Wing Commander Fowler Gobeil, who was one of the Siskin Aerobatic Flight pilots, described the machine as a "fierce little rasper" with a "threshing machine of a motor," referring to its 420 hp Armstrong Siddeley Jaguar, one of the earliest of two-row radial engines. With many of its moving parts exposed, the Jaguar was a very "busy" powerplant, but a reliable one; W/C Gobeil could recall no instances of engine failure with the Siskins.

The Siskin Aerobatic Flight travelled across Canada with the Trans-Canada Air Pageant of 1931, putting on polished displays of tight formation aerobatics, sometimes with the aircraft tied together. With none of the current safety restrictions on airshow performances, Siskin demonstrations were especially exciting, carried out at minimum altitude directly above the crowd. One of the most memorable shows took place at the Cleveland Air Races of that year, when the Siskins appeared by invitation. Although outclassed by their American counterparts flying more modern equipment, the Siskin pilots more than held their own by "laying [their] aircraft in the laps of the spectators in the grandstands," as W/C Gobeil recalled. Beamish, Hawtrey, Harding, Hurley, Howsom, McEwan, McGowan and McNab were the other Siskin Flight pilots.

The RCAF acquired the Siskins brand new from the manufacturer, the first pair of slab-sided Mark IIIs arriving in 1926 for cold weather trials. A further eight of the cleaner Siskin IIIA version, with rounded fuselages, were obtained over the next two years, along with a pair of dual cockpit trainers. The Siskin had its origins in the last months of the First Great War and was developed in the initial postwar generation of RAF fighters, succeeding the wartime S.E. 5As and Snipes. The Siskin III entered RAF service in 1926 and was replaced in the early '30s. Although little used by the RCAF late in the decade, Siskins remained Canada's only fighters until Hurricanes came on strength in 1939.

Robert Bradford's painting enables the viewer to experience the sensation of aerobatic formation flying by placing him in a fourth aircraft with the horizon at the top of the composition and the source of light at the bottom. The variation in markings and the different rudder air-balance on No. 20, the lead aircraft, are noteworthy. This machine also bears the presentation inscription "Lieutenant Arthur Whitten Brown" while No. 59 carries a similar legend recognizing "Captain John Alcock," the other crew member of the trans-Atlantic Vickers Vimy.

45.5 cm x 56.0 cm (18" x 22")
National Aviation Museum

Armstrong Whitworth Siskin – 1930
Robert W. Bradford (1923–   )

Year painted: 1977
Acrylic on canvas

Canadian Vickers Vedette Va

RCAF Civil Operations Flying Boat

Of the many open-cockpit, single-engined flying boats in pre-war use, among the most attractive was the Vedette, designed and built by Canadian Vickers in Montreal. While the type is extinct – modern counterparts such as the Lake Buccaneer are comfortably enclosed – the idea of riding in an open 'canoe with wings' able to alight on any of Canada's myriad of lakes has an appeal somehow not found in contemporary float-equipped machines.

The Vedette was conceived as a forestry patrol aircraft, a successor to the Curtiss HS-2L, which, although ungainly, had served well as the first generation of bush planes. The Vedette was undoubtedly inspired by the accomplishments of the Vickers Viking IVs, which were used civily and by the RCAF. The original civil specifications were adapted by the RCAF to their requirements, and the prototype first flew 6 November 1924, powered by a Rolls-Royce Falcon III of World War I vintage. This engine was soon replaced with much lighter air-cooled radials such as the British Armstrong Siddeley Lynx of 215 hp with which the RCAF was very familiar or, alternately, the American Wright Whirlwind of 215 hp (J5) or 300 hp (J6). Civil purchasers invariably chose the latter.

The Vedette came to represent RCAF activities in pre-war Canada, and also symbolized Canadian flying to air-minded people in other countries. In Robert Bradford's acrylic painting, an RCAF Vedette Va (the last production version) is being test-flown over Canadian Vickers' historic drydock facility on the St Lawrence River. The first Canadian to have his life saved by a parachute and thus become a member of the famed Caterpillar Club was C. S. "Jack" Caldwell. He could not recover from a spin and had to parachute from a Vedette he was testing in May of 1929.

Although the Vedette's wooden hull gradually absorbed water over a season's operation, with an attendant loss of efficiency, the little flying boats were seen from coast to coast in Canada and, on occasion, even beyond the Arctic Circle. RCAF pilots were introduced to seaplane flying on Vedettes, and it has been reported that the front cockpit, usually the post of an aerial photographer, could also accommodate an officer hoping to bring down a goose with his shotgun.

Sixty-one Vedettes were built, of which 44 were for the RCAF and four were exported to Chile. The remainder went to Canadian civil operators. Unfortunately, no Vedettes have survived, although the salvaged remains of a machine are the basis of a reconstruction being undertaken by the Western Canada Aviation Museum.

45.5 cm x 56.0 cm (18" x 22")
National Aviation Museum

Vickers Vedette Va – 1930
Robert W. Bradford (1923–   )

Year painted: c.1963
Acrylic on canvas

The Fairchild FC-2 belonged to the first generation of utility monoplanes that succeeded the HS-2L and other World War I types, adapted as commercial air transports. With the Fokker Universal and Super Universal and the Bellanca Pacemaker, it shared the distinction of being the best known of Canadian bush planes during the 1920s.

The origins of the FC-2 are noteworthy. Its American builder, Sherman Fairchild, had developed a much improved aerial camera and had set up his own firm, Fairchild Aerial Surveys, to fulfill a contract with the Laurentide Paper Company, making use of his new cameras. However, the only aircraft that were available were not designed for aerial photography; operating a camera from an open cockpit was a cold and extremely taxing assignment. To ease the lot of his pilots and photographers, Fairchild decided to build a more suitable aircraft, and he sought the advice of his chief pilot, Ken Saunders, who had flown in the RNAS during the war. They decided upon a high-wing monoplane with large windows in a fully enclosed and heated cabin.

Fairchild returned to New York and engaged engineers Norman McQueen and A. Klemin, who turned these ideas into the FC-1, which first flew in June 1926 powered with the ubiquitous OX-5 engine. ("FC" means Fairchild cabin). A year later, the more modern and practical Wright Whirlwind was fitted, and Fairchild's design became the FC-2. Approximately two dozen were brought into Canada by Western Canada Airways and other operators as well as Fairchild's own firm, which now undertook commercial transport work as well as photography. Canadian Vickers obtained a manufacturing licence from Fairchild and built 12 examples, four for the RCAF, five for civil operators and three as spares. The early FC-2s were known as "Razor-backs" because of their triangular-section rear fuselage. In the Bradford painting opposite, G-CAHL, one of the Razor-backs of the Fairchild Aviation Company (as the company was renamed) that operated out of Grand-Mère, Quebec, in 1927, is shown dropping off a prospecting team. This slab-sided, rather basic appearance was a characteristic of almost all Fairchild utility monoplanes.

Fitted with a Pratt & Whitney Wasp engine of double the power of the Whirlwind, and with six feet of additional span, the FC-2 became the FC-2W. Further enlargement produced the FC-2W-2 with double the payload, and finally the Fairchild 71, some of which remained active until well into the post-World-War-II era. "Punch" Dickins, who had flown a Fokker Universal across the Barrens in 1928, took another party on an even longer flight – 8,700 miles in a Canadian-built 71C. Examples of the FC-2W-2 (G-CART) and of the Model 82 (CF-AXB) of 1936 are to be found in the National Aeronautial Collection. A 71C (CF-AKT) and postwar F-11 Husky, the last of the Fairchild bush planes, reside in the Western Canada Aviation Museum, Winnipeg. Another 71C (CF-ATZ) is in the Alberta Aviation Museum Association at Edmonton.

45.5 cm x 56.0 cm (18" x 22")
National Aviation Museum

Fairchild FC-2 – 1927
Robert W. Bradford (1923–   )

Year painted: 1965
Acrylic on canvas

Fokker Super Universal
A Popular Bush Plane of the '20s

With its clean cantilever wing, long tapered fuselage and cockpit trimly faired into the leading edge of the wing, the Super Universal was regarded as an elegant aircraft. It was a direct development of the Standard Universal as represented initially in Canada by G-CAFU, the first of a dozen "Standards" with Western Canada Airways. The strut bracing of the earlier machine was eliminated; the overall size increased; the formerly open cockpit was enclosed; and with a 400 hp P&W Wasp replacing the 200 hp Wright, power and payload both doubled. Although construction practices were traceable to the Fokker fighters of World War I – notably the steel-tube fuselage construction, the thick high-lift wooden wing and the distinctive rudder shape – responsibility for the design of the Universal from which the "Super" derived, lay with Robert Noorduyn, who later built the Norseman.

The first Super Universal to operate in Canada was G-CARK, acquired by H. A. "Doc" Oaks for Northern Aerial Minerals Exploration Ltd. (NAME) in July 1928. In all, 28 "Supers" saw service here, 18 with WCA and Canadian Airways (as it was renamed following expansion). One of their machines (G-CASK) is seen in Robert Bradford's painting. At the controls was C. H. "Punch" Dickins, the company's manager of flying operations, accompanied by air engineer Bill Nadin. Brand new and gleaming, "SK" is shown on a mineral survey flight of unprecedented length – 3,976 miles – over largely uncharted country. Flying north from Winnipeg to Baker Lake, they swung west to Great Slave Lake before finally returning to their starting point. Sponsoring the trip, which began on 28 August and was completed on 9 September, were Dickins's passengers, mining promoter Colonel C. D. H. MacAlpine and R. Pierce of the *Northern Miner* magazine. This flight, added to his other accomplishments, earned for Punch the McKee Trophy for 1928. Robert Bradford has captured the vast, featureless nature of much of the far north beyond the tree line, where flying has always been a challenge.

A Super Universal owned by the Western Canada Aviation Museum is currently being restored near Calgary, Alberta, by Clark Seaborn, who is also the owner of another historic machine, a Waco UIC Standard cabin biplane of mid-'30s vintage.

45.5 cm x 56.0 cm (18" x 22")
National Aviation Museum

Fokker Super Universal – 1928
Robert W. Bradford (1923–   )

Year painted: 1970
Acrylic on canvas

Stinson SM-1D
Bill Wheeler

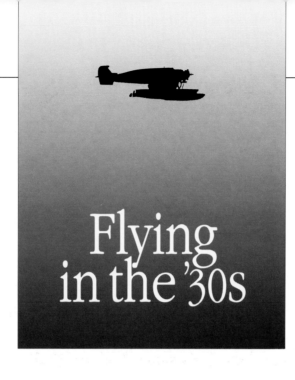

Flying in the '30s

Next to the Fokker and Fairchild series of utility monoplanes, Bellanca CH-300 Pacemakers were the most widely used of pre-war Canadian bush planes. Fifteen were registered in Canada as well as a single, somewhat larger, Skyrocket. Canadian Vickers built six Pacemakers under licence for the RCAF, and Canadian Airways eventually bought four of these, to be included among the above-mentioned civil examples. In the post-World-War-II period, North-West Industries of Edmonton built 13 Senior Skyrockets.

The Pacemaker was a direct descendant of the Bellanca WB-2 *Columbia,* which had been used successfully on two of the first trans-Atlantic flights. Bellancas logged many other record flights. Their popularity with long-distance flyers was no coincidence. It was proven by the Pacemakers' performance commercially; they demonstrated a carrying capacity and range comparable with the more powerful Fokkers and Fairchilds. The six RCAF Pacemakers joined their Fairchilds on aerial survey operations, and pictures taken with their cameras formed the basis of much of the pre-1940s map of Canada.

In appearance, all high-wing Bellancas were identifiable by the sharp downward curve of the upper rear fuselage, approximating a giant airfoil (or wing section) and theoretically providing additional lift. Wing struts were also of airfoil section and wide enough to contribute both lift and stability. The squared wingtips with the corners clipped was another Bellanca feature and one that was carried through the low-wing racers and postwar lightplanes.

The Bellanca was introduced into Canada by A. S. Dawes, who purchased CF-AEC as his personal aircraft. However a close second was W. R. "Wop" May; Bellancas were the principal type flown by his firm, Commercial Airways, which pioneered operations from Edmonton north along the Mackenzie River, as far as the Arctic Ocean. All of Commercial Airways' Pacemakers were sold to Canadian Airways in 1931, and that firm, with nine machines, became the major Canadian operator of the small Bellancas. The other principal Canadian user was General Airways, owned by A. Roy Brown, which operated into northern Quebec from a main base at Rouyn.

Robert Bradford has shown one of General's machines, CF-ATN, taking off after having dropped off a team of prospectors. General Airways flew four Pacemakers and one slightly larger Senior Pacemaker, which, with several smaller Stinson Reliants and other aircraft, comprised their fleet over the years. The firm went out of business prior to the start of the Second World War. "Wop" May and Roy Brown, mentioned above, were the same World War I Camel pilots who were involved with Baron von Richthofen on his last fatal flight.

A Pacemaker obtained in Alaska can be seen in the National Aviation Museum, re-registered as CF-ATN and awaiting more complete restoration. CF-DCE, one of the Senior Skyrockets built postwar by North-West Industries of Edmonton, is being restored by the Canadian Museum of Flight in Surrey, B.C.

Bellanca CH-300 Pacemaker – 1933
Robert W. Bradford (1923–)

45.5 cm x 56.0 cm (18" x 22")
National Aviation Museum

Year painted: c.1965
Acrylic on canvas

In 1964, H. A. "Doc" Oaks, former bush pilot and McKee Trophy winner, observed to this writer that if the Junkers W. 34 were still in production, it would be well able to hold its own against any comparable bush plane. He was referring to an aircraft that had flown as a prototype almost 40 years earlier and had first appeared in Canada in mid-1929.

The W. 34 was an enlarged development of the Junkers F.13 of 1919, which in turn had evolved from the Junkers corrugated aluminum monoplanes of World War I (the J.1 of 1916, the J.9 fighter of 1917 and J.10 of 1918). In an era of wood and fabric biplanes, Dr Hugo Junkers's machines were far in advance of their time. German service pilots were reluctant to accept them and they were not built in quantity.

Four F.13s were imported into Canada, the two most famous being a pair purchased by Imperial Oil to pioneer communication by air along the Mackenzie River to Norman Wells in 1921. They were registered as G-CADQ and G-CADP and christened *René* and *Vic* respectively. After a gallant attempt to complete the lengthy flight, in which both aircraft were damaged and repaired only with consider-

able ingenuity by those involved, the project was abandoned. Aerial operations on the Mackenzie would not be resumed for a further six years.

The first Junkers W. 34 was imported by Western Canada Airways in May of 1929. H. A. Oaks, the firm's original manager, had been responsible for organizing operations in 1927 and had acquired Fokker and Fairchild aircraft as the best available equipment. However, he felt that all-metal aircraft, should they become available, would afford greater serviceability for bush operations. His successor, Leigh Brintnell, agreed with him and placed orders for the German machines, the first of which actually came from Sweden. Oaks himself purchased a W. 34 (CF-AQV) for his own Oaks Airways, which he founded after leaving WCA. In all, a total of nine W. 33/34s came to Canada and served for an average of over 15 years, amply proving the correctness of the "all-metal" preference. There were two variants: the W. 33 with a water-cooled Junkers in-line engine of 310 hp, and the W. 34 with various air-cooled radial engines such as the 420 hp P&W Wasp. The two Canadian W. 33s were eventually converted to W. 34s

with the installation of the American engines.

Among their contemporaries, the W. 34s stood out because of their corrugated aluminum skin and low-wing configuration. While the latter feature caused docking problems in summer, in winter it could prevent the aircraft from sinking should the ice give way beneath the aircraft's skis, an all-too-common occurrence. The roomy cabin, rugged construction and clean design allowed the Junkers to outperform all competition and more than compensated for the greater initial cost. Rex Terpening, an air engineer with Canadian Airways, referred to the W. 34 as the "Cadillac of bush planes" and this sentiment has been echoed by many others.

The last W. 34 to arrive in Canada, CF-ATF, originally of Canadian Airways, was repurchased in 1962 from the then-owners by Mrs J. A. Richardson, widow of the firm's founder, and donated to the National Aviation Museum, a fitting end to 30 years of productive flying. Tom Bjarnason's restrained pastel rendering, prepared as cover art for the *Journal* of the Canadian Aviation Historical Society, depicts 'ATF fitted with floats for summer operation.

30.0 cm x 27.3 cm (11 ¾" x 10 ¾")
Collection of the artist

Junkers W. 33/34 – 1934
Tom Bjarnason (1925–   )

Year painted: 1986
Pastel on board

Curtiss-Reid Rambler
Canada's First Production Light Aircraft

The exploits of Canada's World War I pilots captured the imagination of young people – and of the not-so-young. Few Canadian cities did not support flying clubs and schools. The surplus JN-4 Canucks that had been the original equipment for these enterprises soon began to show their age, and their operators wanted more modern replacements. This was met largely by de Havilland D.H. 60 Cirrus and Gipsy Moths, built in England and erected at the firm's Downsview (Toronto) Canadian branch. There were also a few examples of the contemporary Avro Avian and Fleet 2. The federal government saw the value of the flying clubs as sources of trained pilots who would be vital should Canada ever again go to war, and, to encourage the movement, the government made aircraft available. Each machine that a club purchased was matched by another donated by the government.

At this time, Wilfrid Reid, who had been a designer with Canadian Vickers, left that firm and formed his own Reid Aircraft Company to design and build a new light training machine – a Canadian product for a Canadian market. The result was a very attractive aircraft with traditional open cockpits in tandem and a distinctive sesquiplane wing arrangement. Power was provided initially by an 80 hp Cirrus engine (later replaced with a 100 hp Gipsy) while construction was entirely of metal with fabric covering. In Septembr 1928, Martin Berlyn test-flew the first rambler (G-CAVO) at Montreal's Cartierville Airport. Before the end of the year, an American firm, the Curtiss Aeroplane and Motor Company, purchased the Reid Company, creating the new Curtiss-Reid Aircraft Co. Ltd. and making available the necessary capital for expansion.

The Rambler III (CF-ACI) in Robert Bradford's painting was owned by the Montreal Light Aeroplane Club and is shown with well-known aviation historian Ken Molson at the controls soloing for his private pilot's licence in 1936. The painting was presented by the staff of the National Aviation Museum (including the artist, as assistant curator) to Ken upon his retirement as curator in 1967.

In all, Reid and Curtiss-Reid built 43 Ramblers between 1928 and 1937: nine for the RCAF, six exported and the remainder sold privately in Canada. Ramblers were well liked but, unfortunately, no examples are known to exist today. Perhaps one of the many aviation museums that are springing up across Canada will undertake the construction of a replica.

50.0 cm x 60.0 cm (19 ½" x 23 ½")
Ken Molson

Rambler Solo – 1936
Robert W. Bradford (1923–   )

Year painted: 1967
Oil on canvas

de Havilland D.H. 80A Puss Moth

Preferred for Long-Distance Flights

The history of aviation records numerous occasions when an outstanding aircraft's origins are to be found in an earlier unsuccessful design. One example is the Puss Moth, a scaled down version of the overweight and inefficient D.H. 75 Hawk Moth. Although only a handful of Hawk Moths were built and the type soon disappeared, the "Puss" enjoyed a long and often spectacular career.

The popularity of the D.H. 60 series of two-place light biplanes lead the de Havilland firm to conclude that a successor with more comfortably enclosed passenger accommodation would gain still wider acceptance. Adopting a high-wing monoplane configuration and using the same Gipsy engine, but inverting it to improve the pilot's view, they produced an aeroplane of unexpected efficiency. Not only did the D.H. 80 carry an additional passenger, it was appreciably faster than its predecessor. To reduce power-off speed on landing approaches, the streamlined landing struts could be turned 90 degrees to act as air brakes.

The pilot sat alone in front of the side-by-side but slightly staggered passenger seats. In an era of long-distance flying, the Puss Moth's capabilities were not overlooked and it tallied numerous record-setting flights, with additional fuel tanks in place of passenger seating. Jim Mollison, among its most notable pilots, made the first solo east-west Atlantic crossing in August 1932, one of his many accomplishments.

The all-wood prototype D.H. 80 first flew on 9 September 1929. A few months later the production version (the D.H. 80A) with a steel tube fuselage, recorded its first flight. An early production machine CF-AGO was sent to Canada from England and flown from Toronto to Vancouver and back on a successful demonstration tour. De Havilland's Canadian branch immediately began assembling British-built components to fill Canadian orders: 33 Puss Moths were sold in Canada, almost evenly split between the RCAF and civil operators. Of this total, several bore both civil and military markings at different times. H. J. L. "Bert" Hinkler supervised the erection and modification of a Puss Moth (CF-APK) at DHC for long-distance flying and used it on an epic flight to South America then across the South Atlantic to Africa and finally north to England.

From June 1931 until early in 1934 the Puss Moth CF-IOL (shown opposite) was flown by well-known bush pilot T. M. "Pat" Reid. Reid was aviation sales manager for Imperial Oil. In 1931, he flew the firm's newly acquired Puss Moth as tour leader of the Trans-Canada Air Pageant, making a return trans-continental flight with stops all across the continent. There were few parts of Canada not visited by Reid and his Puss Moth while promoting the use of his employer's products. Distinguished Canadian illustrator Huntley Brown has depicted the Puss Moth high above a wintery Mackenzie Delta. This painting appeared originally in the *Imperial Oil Review*. The artist's treatment is typically broad and painterly.

Only a single Puss Moth exists today in Canada, a machine brought from England in 1970 by the Rev John MacGillivray, who was then an RCAF chaplain. He sold it to the National Aviation Museum in 1976. It bears the registration CF-PEI and is painted red and silver, the colours of a Puss Moth owned and flown by Mrs Louise Jenkins of Charlottetown in 1932.

50.7 cm x 91.5 cm (20" x 36")
Collection of the author

Pat Reid's Puss Moth – 1932
Huntley Brown (1932–   )

Year painted: 1980
Acrylic on canvas

Curtiss-Reid Courier

Diminutive Mail Carrier

To make the carrying of airmail a more viable proposition in the midst of the Depression, John A. D. McCurdy, managing director of Curtiss-Reid Aviation of Montreal, proposed a relatively small and low-powered aircraft tailored expressly for transporting mail. R. N. Bell, formerly of Canadian Vickers, designed the new machine called the Courier, which flew for the first time in January 1932 with "Pete" Vachon at the controls. This single-place parasol monoplane was one of the most attractive aircraft of its day. The pilot occupied an open cockpit behind the mail compartment located in the forward fuselage. The Courier was appreciably smaller than the biplanes such as the Stearman 4EM and the Fairchild cabin monoplanes that were then carrying mail and, with a 120 hp Gipsy III engine, required roughly a quarter of the power.

Unfortunately, Canadian Airways, who had possessed the bulk of the airmail contracts prior to cancellation, were not interested in the Courier. Gath Edwards, who flew it on the Maritime Air Tour later in the year, described it as a very pleasant aircraft to fly. But without a customer, no further production was considered. A. Algarson of Montreal purchased the Courier in February 1933 and turned it over to Fairchild Aviation for modifications, which included a large gas tank fitted into the mail compartment. Obviously the aircraft was being fitted for a long-distance flight attempt. But what this was to be, Algarson never disclosed; the aircraft was destroyed in a test flight at Longueuil in June of 1933, killing the pilot Bernard Martin.

Robert Bradford has shown the bright red Courier as it appeared when first flown. Below its wings is the Curtiss-Reid facility at Cartierville airport. The original painting is scarcely larger than the reproduction and was done as a preliminary study for a National Aviation Museum painting that was proposed but never executed. Bradford's treatment of his subject is much freer than is customary with his final studio pieces. The original is in the possession of Ken Molson whose research has provided most of the foregoing data.

With its diminutive 21-foot length, 30-foot span and its clean lines, the Courier would seem to represent an ideal construction project for the more sophisticated homebuilder of aircraft. Suitable engines are available and a replica of the Courier would more than hold its own among such homebuilts as the Sky Bolt, Star Duster and Eagle, which recall the sleek fighter aircraft of an earlier day.

12.0 cm x 25.5 cm (4 3/4" x 10")
Ken Molson

Curtiss-Reid Courier – 1932
Robert W. Bradford (1923–   )

Year painted: c.1964
Acrylic on board

Bellanca Aircruiser

A Giant among Bush Planes

Although not the largest aircraft to operate in the pre-war Canadian North – that distinction went to the Junkers Ju. 52/1m (CF-ARM) owned by Canadian Airways – the Bellanca Aircruiser was a close runner-up. With its distinctive auxilliary wing (or lifting struts), there was no mistaking an Aircruiser for any other aircraft, and the type soon became known as the "Flying W" – for obvious reasons. The Aircruiser grew out of a specially designed long-distance machine, the Bellanca K, of 1928, named the *Roma* (later *Enna Jettick*) which could carry fuel sufficient for a flight of 12,000 miles non-stop. A development, the 12-passenger P-200 Airbus, was introduced in 1932 and was favourably received in spite of the depressed times, with 14 ordered by the US Army Air Service.

The first of the improved Aircruiser variant to be seen in Canada was CF-AWR, painted by Robert Bradford, being loaded with uranium ore concentrate on a frosty morning at Great Bear Lake, about 1937, for the trip to Edmonton. Standing in the foreground is S. R. "Stan" McMillan, the pilot of 'AWR. Leigh Brintnell, the well-known founder of Mackenzie Air Service, had purchased 'AWR new in early 1935 expressly for this contract, and her performance was such that he eventually acquired two additional Aircruisers, CF-BKV and CF-BTW. Another Aircruiser, CF-BLT, was active in the Yukon, and a single elderly P-200 Airbus was flown only briefly in Canada before being written off in a crash.

In 1943, Canadian Pacific Airlines purchased the Mackenzie Air Service Aircruisers 'BKV and 'BTW and subsequently resold them to smaller operators. 'AWR had gone to Canadian Airways four years earlier. Both 'AWR and 'BKV were lost in non-fatal crashes. But the last survivor, CF-BTW, was to remain in operation until 1990, when she was sold in the United States after a half-century of service. Fortunately, the remains of CF-AWR had been recovered in 1971, after 24 years in the bush, by a crew from the Western Canada Aviation Museum, and she is now undergoing a painstaking restoration with parts from CF-BKV.

In their spacious cabins, which could accommodate loads too bulky for smaller machines, the Aircruisers could carry a payload of well over two tons, or an equivalent weight in passengers and their gear. In summer the "Big Bellancas" flew with giant 30-foot floats, and, in winter, with outsize skis. Only during spring or fall changeovers were the Aircruisers, like all bush types, ever fitted with wheels. Up front were Wright Cyclone or Pratt & Whitney Hornet engines in the 700 hp range. With their smaller kin, the Pacemakers and Skyrockets, they shared the deep slab-sided fuselage of airfoil profile that was a Bellanca trademark.

49.5 cm x 64.5 cm (19$\frac{1}{2}$" x 25$\frac{1}{2}$")
Collection of the artist

The Big Bellanca – **1937**
Robert W. Bradford (1923–   )

Year painted: 1989
Acrylic on canvas

In the more than half a century since the Norseman prototype CF-AYO was first test-flown by Jack McDonough in November 1935, R. B. C. "Bob" Noorduyn's utility transport has gained an enviable reputation. In Canada some four dozen Norseman aircraft still remain airworthy, and they have seen service in many countries over a span of years, well beyond that of most fabric-covered aircraft. Having designed Anthony Fokker's Universal, Bob Noorduyn was familiar with utility monoplanes.

From the outset, the Norseman was intended as a bush plane, the first Canadian machine designed as such, incorporating sugestions from pilots experienced in northern operations. With its rotund and roomy fuselage, cleanly cowled engine and overall streamlining, the Norseman represented an obvious advance over its angular predecessors. The prototype (and sole Mark I) and three Mark IIs were all powered by the Wright Whirlwind with 420 hp. The builders soon realized that more power was needed, and all subsequent aircraft were fitted with Pratt & Whitney Wasps of 550 and 600 hp. Only a few examples were built before World War II curtailed civilian sales, and all further production was devoted to the military. The US Army Air Corps became the major customer, acquiring over 800 UC and YC-64s, and the RCAF purchased 100 Norsemans of various models. With surplus military aircraft so readily available after 1945, only a handful of additional Norseman aircraft have been built since then.

CF-AZE, shown by Robert Bradford as she skims low over a prospecting crew, was a Mark II built in 1936 and purchased and flown by Robert Cockeram, himself a prospector and founder of Prospector Airways Limited. Like so many in his field, Cockeram had recognized the value of aircraft in mining exploration. And with its rugged construction, the Norseman was well suited to bush operation. On skis or floats, pilots used it in every corner of the Canadian North. Later, it worked alongside the smaller de Havilland DHC-2 Beaver and the larger DHC-3 Otter.

Numerous examples of the type are to be found in museums, most notably CF-BSC, a Mark IV which was flown by the late Thurston ("Rusty") Blakey of Austin Airways for 40 years and is now in the Canadian Museum of Flight in Vancouver. CF-SAM, formerly of the Saskatchewan Government Air Service, is in the Western Development Museum at Saskatoon, and an ex-RCAF machine is in the NAM. Still operating commercially out of Ignace, Ontario, is CF-DTL, a Mark V owned and flown by Gord Hughes. Other examples are under restoration.

45.5 cm x 56.0 cm (18" x 22")
National Aviation Museum

Noorduyn Norseman II – 1936
Robert W. Bradford (1923–   )

Year painted: 1979
Acrylic on canvas

Lockheed 10A Electra

Airliner and Record Setter

The Lockheed Electra was a worthy successor to the renowned aircraft which preceeded it, the exceedingly clean Vega with its advanced construction of wooden monocoque, the parasol Air Express, and low-wing Sirius, Altair and Orion derivatives. The *Winnie Mae*, in which Wiley Post twice set records circling the globe, undoubtedly became the most famous of Vegas. But the single-engined Lockheeds were also flown by such storied names as Charles Lindbergh, Amelia Earhart, Roscoe Turner, Frank Hawkes, Jimmy Doolittle and Sir Charles Kingsford-Smith.

The twin-engined Electra grew out of the need for a multi-engined airliner when US government legislation in the late '30s forbade the use of single-engined aircraft in scheduled airline service.

The first Electra to see service in Canada was purchased in August 1936 by Canadian Airways to fly their Vancouver-Seattle mail and passenger run. While they owned the mail contract, the passengers they hoped to attract had shown only scant interest in flying in their de Havilland Dragon Rapide twin-engined biplane. Travellers preferred to fly in the faster and more modern Boeing 247 which United Airlines used on the route. The introduction of the 10A, CF-AZY, set the matter right. Later the same month, Canadian Airways bought a second Electra, CF-BAF, to be leased by the Government of Canada to survey routes for the new Canadian trans-continental airline, which was soon to be formed. Canadian Airways were strong contenders to operate such a line.

Once the route investigation had been completed, Canadian Airways placed 'BAF on a run from Winnipeg to the booming gold-mining town of Red Lake, Ontario, fitting the aircraft with streamlined Lockheed skis and operating from the frozen ice of the lake. Z. L. "Lewie" Leigh flew the aircraft. But the Lockheed served only briefly in Canadian Airways' colours; when Trans-Canada Air Lines was created – as a crown corporation without the involvement of Canadian Airways – TCA purchased the two Lockheeds ('AZY and 'BAF) and bought three more new from Lockheed: CF-TCA, CF-TCB and CF-TCC, which comprised their initial passenger fleet.

It is one of these machines which Robert Bradford has shown in *Time Warp*, commissioned by Air Canada to mark their 50th anniversary. CF-TCC has just left the ground, in the looming presence of one of her successors, an Air Canada Boeing 767. The crew and passengers – from 1937 – are as astonished by the mighty 767 (which would not enter the "Company's" service for another 46 years) as the pilot and co-pilot of the 767. Where the Electra could carry 10 passengers, the 767 carries up to 262 – and weighs more than 30 Electras.

TCA soon replaced CF-TCC and their other Electras with larger and more powerful Lockheed 14 Super Electras, and turned the smaller machines over to the RCAF for communications duties. Postwar, they were flown by a succession of civil operators. On two occasions, Air Canada re-acquired 'TCC to make trans-Canada flights: in 1962, on the firm's 25th anniversary, when it was leased from its Canadian operator, and again in 1984 when it was purchased from a US owner. Air Canada completely rebuilt 'TCC for the 1986 "Sentimental Journey" 50th anniversary celebrations. Previously, in 1968, Air Canada also bought the former CF-TCA and donated it to the National Aviation Museum. The previous year, it had been flown on a round-the-world flight in memory of Amelia Earhart – 30 years after her disappearance over the Pacific in a similar machine. 'TCC, the last airworthy Lockheed 10A, can be seen in the Western Canada Aviation Museum when not on her annual summer display flight program.

55.5 cm x 102.0 cm (22" x 40")
Air Canada

Time Warp – 1937
Robert W. Bradford (1923–   )

Year painted: 1987
Oil on canvas

Heath Parasol
Popular Homebuilt of the '30s

The idea of building and flying one's own aeroplane has always been intriguing and exciting. Beginning with the Wrights, the earliest aviators had constructed almost all their own machines. This practice, interrupted only by two wars, has steadily gained momentum. Today, most airports have their quota of highly sophisticated homebuilt aircraft.

In 1929, the magazine *Popular Aviation and Aeronautics* began publishing a series of articles detailing the construction of the small but sturdy single-place Heath Parasol, which could be built by anyone with sufficient ambition and determination. The parasol configuration, evolved during World War I, combined a single wing with a fuselage hung beneath it from struts. Many young men accepted the challenge, including Fred Hotson, then a high school student in Fergus, Ontario. Building his Heath was to occupy most of Fred's spare time for the next eight years, through the remainder of his high school career, an aviation technology course in Toronto, and his first years at de Havilland as an apprentice.

The wings, transported from Fergus to Toronto, were rebuilt, and a basic steel-tube fuselage was purchased from another would-be Heath builder. With the addition of a deeper turtle deck, a head rest, an enlarged windshield and the lines of the tailplane "sweetened," it bore slight resemblance to the 20 or so other Canadian-built Heaths. The linen covering was sewn on by the ladies from de Havilland's fabric shop, and the doping was carried out by Fred, assisted by two men later to become well known in Canadian aviation circles: George Neal and Don Murray. With the wings braced by Puss Moth struts, modified from obsolete de Havilland stock, the little Parasol emerged as a very attractive aeroplane, "the best homebuilt" he had seen, according to Colonel Doug Joy of the Department of Transport. Fred then obtained the registration CF-BLS.

The little Parasol took to the air for her maiden flight on 9 October 1938 with Toronto Flying Club instructor Allan Bishop in the cockpit. The proud builder and his helpers were pleased to learn that only the most minor adjustments were needed.

In the painting opposite, I have shown 'BLS early in her career over the Toronto Flying Club. The powerplant, a modified four-cylinder Henderson motorcycle engine of 23 hp, ran very smoothly. But Fred's "mods" had added weight to the airframe, and the need for more power was apparent. A 32 hp ABC Scorpion that had once powered a Glenny-Henderson Gadfly was obtained from Professor Tom Loudon of the University of Toronto. With it, the Heath became a delight to fly. Unfortunately Fred and his friends were only able to log 27 hours in the air before the Heath had to be placed in storage. Canada was at war, and Fred was posted away from Toronto as an Air Observer School instructor. Sadly, the Heath never flew again and was eventually broken up.

34.5 cm x 48.3 cm (13 ½" x 19")
Fred W. Hotson

Fred Hotson's Heath – 1938
William Wheeler (1931–   )

Year painted: 1966
Gouache on board

Hawker Typhoons of 198 Squadron, RAF
Les Waller

World War II

Vickers Wellington
The Fondly Remembered Wimpy

The Wellington was in many ways ahead of its time. Designed to a set of 1932 specifications, it first flew in July 1936 as the most advanced RAF heavy bomber of the day, comparing favourably with similar aircraft from any nation. It embodied a radically new method of geodetic construction that had been evolved by B. N. (later Sir Barnes) Wallis – a widely woven mesh or basket-weave of riveted aluminum strips formed not only the fuselage but wing and tail surfaces as well. The skin of the Wellington thus displayed a distinctive oblique grid texture. But the resultant structure possessed strength and amazing flexibility at a time when rigidity was the norm. It was capable of absorbing battle damage that would have proved fatal to aeroplanes of conventional design. Exactly 11,461 Wellingtons were built but only one has been preserved – in the RAF Bomber Command Museum at Hendon, England. Another Wellington has been raised from the depths of Loch Ness, but is unlikely to be restored after being immersed in salt water for so long.

Like the Spitfire, the Wellington possessed great 'stretch'. Built throughout the war, it progressed through successive Marks fitted with ever bigger engines: the Mark I with 1,050 Pegasus, the Mark II with 1,145 hp Merlins, the Mark III with 1,375 Hercules, the Mark IV with 1,200 hp P&W Twin Wasps and, finally, the superlative Mark X with 1,675 hp Hercules. When the first 1,000-bomber raid was launched on Germany, over half of the aircraft used were Wellingtons. In the early years of the bomber offensive, the "Wimpy" (it was nicknamed after the hamburger-loving "J. Wellington Wimpy" from the popular *Popeye* comic strip) was the backbone of Bomber Command. It proved capable of carrying the 4,000-lb "Blockbuster" bombs or "cookies" as they were called by airmen. The first ones fell on Emden in 1941.

When the four-engined 'heavies' such as the Halifax and Lancaster took over the night-bombing role, the Wellington assumed other important duties: the training of aircrew on operational training units (OTUs), precision bombing in North Africa, and coastal patrol. A Coastal Command Wellington X from 407 Squadron RCAF is shown taking off from RAF Chivenor on 8 January 1945 in Charles Goldhamer's bold watercolour. Goldhamer, in common with most of Canada's other official war artists, preferred watercolour for work in the field. He was one of the most accomplished with the medium and he was also a fine draughtsman.

19.7 cm x 22.2 cm (8" x 9")
Canadian War Museum

Take-Off – 1945
Charles Goldhamer (1903–1985)

Year painted: 1945
Watercolour

Hawker Hurricane
Battle of Britain Mainstay

The Hawker Hurricane will always be remembered for its role in the Battle of Britain during the summer of 1940, when it bore the brunt of the fighting, substantially outnumbering the Spitfire with which it shared honours. Whenever possible, Hurricanes were used against the Luftwaffe's Heinkels, Dorniers and Junkers. Spitfires, with their superior climb and speed, engaged the Messerschmitt Bf 109s flying cover for the bombers. The only RCAF squadron to take part was 401 lead by S/L Gordon McGregor. Earlier, 242 Squadron, an RAF unit commanded by S/L Fowler Gobeil (a former Siskin pilot) with a large complement of Canadians, had flown their Hurricanes in a retreating action across France and at Dunkirk. Hurricanes served throughout World War II.

Although their usefulness as fighters soon diminished, they were stable and strongly built 'gun platforms'. Fitted with larger engines and four 20-mm cannon, they became effective ground-attack aircraft. Some Hurricanes were used against tanks, with two 40-mm cannon in pods hung beneath the wings, while others were fitted with racks for two 500-lb bombs as "Hurribombers." Still others were equipped to launch rockets. Hurricanes fought all around the world, from Burma to Russia, and were even flown off aircraft carriers to reach Norway and Malta. A few were catapulted from the decks of merchant ships to intercept the Luftwaffe's long-range Focke Wulf Fw 200 Condors that preyed on convoys far out in the Atlantic. If they could not reach shore, the pilots ditched their machines or bailed out to be picked up, with luck.

The prototype Hurricane flew for the first time in November 1935 and began life as the "Fury Monoplane," reflecting its descent from that most elegant of biplane fighters. With its thick wing and seeming bulk, it lacked the Fury's delicate grace, taking on instead a more purposeful character. In place of the traditional paired machine guns, the Hurricane carried eight and, for ease of construction, it employed the same steel, aluminum and fabric construction as its biplane predecessor.

Well over 14,000 Hurricanes were built, 1,457 of them in Canada by the Canadian Car and Foundry in Fort William (now Thunder Bay). A number of Hurricanes have been preserved in Canada, notably a former CC&F-built RCAF machine regularly flown by the Canadian Warplane Heritage of Hamilton, Ontario. Others are to be found in the National Aviation Museum, Ottawa, and in the Reynolds Aviation Museum at Wetaskiwin, Alberta. In Surrey, near Vancouver, the Canadian Museum of Flight and Transportation is restoring another example.

The accompanying painting was created by the author as a book jacket illustration. It displays the vigorous brushwork that was popular with illustrators of the '60s. The Hurricanes, Canadian Mark Xs, are intended to be typical and do not represent any particular unit. The squadron code LA, which they bear, was set aside for the next Canadian fighter unit that would have been formed had World War II continued. It was never used.

28.0 cm x 40.0 cm (11" x 15 ½")
Collection of the artist

Hurricanes Attacking – 1941
William Wheeler (1931–   )

Year painted: 1965
Gouache on board

Avro Anson I

A Gentleman's Aeroplane

Few aircraft are as fondly remembered by pilots as the Avro Anson. While "Faithful Annie" had faults, most notably a noisy and very draughty "greenhouse" in all Marks up to the V, her forgiving nature more than compensated. The seeming dignity with which she, when allowed to, would overcome a trainee's heavy handedness confirmed her reputation as a "gentleman's aeroplane." Beginning life in 1935 as a twin-engined civil transport, the Avro 652 was a low-winged development of the tri-motored Fokker F.VII-3m for which A. V. Roe held a manufacturing licence. The RAF needed just such a machine for coastal patrol duties, and the light twin was soon modified for its new role.

When war broke out, the first "kill" accorded the RAF was a Dornier Do 18 flying boat brought down by a Coastal Command Anson. Other Ansons, although grossly outclassed, bested such high-performance enemy aircraft as the Messerschmitt Bf 109 and Me 110. The Anson's very ability to fly slowly proved an advantage.

When the British Commonwealth Air Training Plan was initiated in 1939, the Anson was selected as the principal twin-engined trainer, and the RCAF was eventually to have some 4,413 on strength. More than 20,000 pilots trained on them, as well as thousands of gunners, navigators and bomb aimers.

Shown in Jim Bruce's meticulous acrylic painting is a British-built Anson I, RCAF 6102, operated by No. 2 Air Observer School at Edmonton, Alberta. The flat prairie terrain seen below and the predictable weather proved ideal for training.

The Anson I could be recognized by the engine cowlings with distinctive helmets over each cylinder head, a characteristic of the 335 hp Armstrong Siddeley Cheetahs which powered it. Later Marks were fitted with the 330 hp Jacobs L6MB, the 450 hp Wright Whirlwind and finally the 450 hp Pratt & Whitney Wasp Junior. The latter powered the Mark V, which was a distinctly Canadian version with a considerably more streamlined, moulded plywood fuselage, and round ports in place of the original extensive plexiglass. With this machine, most of the original faults had been eliminated, and its performance substantially improved. Large numbers of Anson Vs were sold as surplus to commercial operators and gave useful service for as long as 30 years.

The staff of the Western Development Museum at Saskatoon have completed the restoration of an Anson I, so far a unique exhibit. An Anson V is currently flown by the Canadian Warplane Heritage at Mount Hope, Ontario, and others are on display in the Commonwealth Air Training Plan Museum at Brandon, Manitoba, and in the National Aviation Museum.

35.5 cm x 33.7 cm (14" x 13¼")
Canadian Aviation Historical Society

Avro Anson I – **1940**
Jim Bruce (1932–   )

Year painted: 1971
Acrylic on board

Vickers Supermarine Spitfire

Too Beautiful to be a Warplane

Has there ever been a more famous aeroplane than the Spitfire? Ever since it was flown so valiantly in the Battle of Britain, the Supermarine fighter has captured and held public imagination. While there were almost half again as many Hurricanes in that historic conflict and they destroyed the lion's share of enemy aircraft, the Spitfire somehow received the greater recognition. It is easy to speculate as to why. No aircraft has ever possessed more aesthetically pleasing lines than the Spitfire, which has been described as a piece of sculpture, too beautiful to be a warplane. It was small and seemingly delicate, with the slimmest possible fuselage behind its cleanly cowled Rolls-Royce Merlin. But its most distinctive feature was a graceful semi-elliptical wing. The Spitfire's designer, Reginald Mitchell, died in 1937.

Like its contemporary, the Hurricane, the Spitfire came of distinguished lineage. It was built to a 1934 Air Ministry specification for a monoplane fighter able to carry eight guns and utilize a new V-12 Rolls-Royce engine developed from the "sprint" engines used so successfully in the Schneider Trophy racers. Indeed the Spitfire itself had evolved from the Supermarine S-6 and S-6B machines which had captured the prestigious trophy outright

for Britain, although the resemblance was superficial. The Schneider Trophy, an international award, went annually to the winner of a race for seaplanes, with the first sequential triple victor to retain the cup permanently. Many world air speed records were set during these competitions.

"Mutt" Summers flew the prototype Spitfire in March 1936, demonstrating a performance capability that resulted in an immediate order of 300 machines for the RAF. Spitfires remained in production until late 1947 by which time 20,334 had been built. They were still in front-line service as late as 1954. In addition, there were over 1,200 Seafires. Development progressed steadily through no less than 24 variants; obviously the design possessed great 'stretch' potential. While the Spitfire was always a universally liked pilots' aeroplane and a superlative dog-fighter, it was fitted with ever-more-powerful engines and adapted for such roles as photo-reconnaissance and fighter bomber, as well as low-, medium- and high-level intercepter. In 1943, the Merlin-powered versions were joined by variants powered with the heavier and more powerful Rolls-Royce Griffin. Where the prototype had achieved 360 mph on 990 hp, the fastest Spitfire was the high-flying and un-

armed Mark XIX, which reached 460 mph with a 2,050 hp Griffin. Total weight increased from 5,332 lb to almost five tons and, while the last variants were obviously Spitfires, they were very different machines from those that had fought in 1939.

Ten RCAF squadrons flew Spitfires, mostly Marks V and IX and, following the Normandy invasion, a Canadian Spitfire wing led by W/C Johnny Johnson was very prominent. Many more Canadians flew Spitfires with RAF units, and the type was used around the globe in every theatre of war. Don Anderson, an official war artist and subsequently a leading Canadian illustrator, created the accompanying painting of 416 "City of Oshawa" Squadron Spitfires flying low over the Channel. The lead aircraft is flown by F/L J. A. "Jackie" Rae, DFC, who was later to form the very popular Spitfire Band.

The National Aviation Museum owns three Spitfires – a Mark II, IX and a XVI. The latter machine is on loan to the Western Canada Aviation Museum in Winnipeg. A Mark V is being restored by a group lead by Don Campbell of Kapuskasing, Ontario, and the Canadian Warplane Heritage of Hamilton, Ontario, is rebuilding a Seafire.

51 cm x 76 cm (20" x 30")
Collection of the artist

Spitfires of 416 Squadron – 1943
Don Anderson (1920–)

Year painted: 1985
Acrylic on board

The Harvard – or Texan or SNJ – in its various Marks is credited with training more pilots than any other single type of aircraft, probably due to its supreme suitability for the job. Hence the lengthy period it remained in service – some two decades with the RCAF. It proved an ideal tool for honing the skills of novice pilots fresh from such primary trainers as the Tiger Moth, Finch or Cornell to a level that would allow them to handle WW II high-performance fighters and, later, first-generation jets. Few pilots who completed their training on Harvards do not have fond memories of the exhilaration and satisfaction that came with mastering the snarling "Yellow Peril."

The type had its origins in the North American NA-16 of 1936, the firm's first design and the first of a confusing multiplicity of variants. The Harvard was chosen in 1939 as the sole advanced single-engine trainer for the British Commonwealth Air Training Plan. The Fleet 60 Fort had been designed for the role but did not have the necessary performance and was relegated to use as a radio and navigational trainer. The first of 34 Harvard 1s, identified by a fabric-covered rear fuselage and rounded rudder, was obtained in July 1939. Harvard 2s, the dominant variant with the characteristic triangular vertical tail, began coming on strength in 1940 until there were nearly 1,800, sufficient to equip 12 Service Flying Training Schools (SFTS). One unusual machine was an NA-44, based at Trenton and looking much like a Harvard but with a blue fuselage and a Wright Cyclone engine of 850 hp. The additional horses apparently gave it a performance edge on the Harvards with their 600 hp Wasps, and as the "CO's Jeep," it was reserved for use by senior officers.

Sometimes mistaken for Harvards were the 119 NA-64 Yales, which were taken over from French contracts prior to the occupation of that country. Powered by the 400 hp Wright Whirlwind and with a fixed undercarriage, their performance was found inadequate for advanced training; flying one has been compared to operating a Harvard on half-power with the undercarriage down. Like the Forts, they too became wireless trainers.

About 2,800 Harvard 2s were built in Canada by Noorduyn Aviation of Montreal between 1942 and 1945, and in 1951, during the Korean War, the type was returned to production – as the Harvard 4 – by the Canadian Car and Foundry at Fort William (now Thunder Bay), Ontario, and a further 550 were built. Beside their spartan wartime counterparts, the Mark 4s impressed those who trained on them as the embodiment of luxury. They can be identified by their simplified canopy structure. More Harvards have been built in Canada than any other type of aircraft. Tom Bjarnason's pastel painting, originally a cover for the *Journal* of the Canadian Aviation Historical Society, depicts a selection of Harvards flown at RCAF Dunnville Service Flying Training School, one of the stations where World War II fighter pilots were introduced to fighter-like aircraft.

Civilian Harvards are still to be found in quantity; they appear regularly at airshows, occasionally flying in formations, and most air museums boast examples.

53.4 cm x 46.9 cm (21" x 18½")
Collection of the artist

Dunnville Harvards – 1941
Tom Bjarnason (1925–   )

Year painted: 1989
Pastel on board

Douglas DC-3

Greatest Airliner Ever

The DC-3, which first flew in December 1935 and went out of production in 1945, is still in wide use well over a half-century later, a record matched by no other aircraft. In fact it has outlasted most of those aircraft that were built to replace it. Such amazing longevity must undoubtedly be attributed not only to the excellence of the original design but to its rugged construction. "Over-built" is the term most often used to describe DC-3 structure.

The DC-3 grew out of a request by American Airlines to redesign the highly successful DC-2 as an aerial equivalent of the railway sleeper car. The result was the DST – Douglas Skysleeper Transport – which could provide beds for 14 passengers on overnight flights or seat twice that number for shorter daylight trips. In the years prior to World War II, DC-3s entered airline sevice as fast as Douglas could build them. Their efficient operation made air transport a paying proposition for the airlines fortunate enough to obtain them.

With the outbreak of war, the DC-3, as the best transport available, became a key aircraft in the air forces of all the Allied nations. In the USAAC and USAAF, it received the designation C-47 (as well as C-48, -49, -50, -51, -52 and -53) and was also known as the Sky Train and Sky Trooper. But it is probably best remembered by its RAF name of Dakota or by its nickname of "Gooney Bird." Robert Bradford has shown unarmed Dakotas of 435 Squadron RCAF dropping supplies to Allied troops at Shwebo in Burma on 12 January 1945, an extremely dangerous mission in view of the lack of fighter escort. Two of the Dakota pilots who successfully evaded the attacks of the Nakajima "Oscar" fighters of the Japanese Army were awarded the Distinguished Flying Cross. The painting was commissioned by the 435/436 Burma Star Squadrons' Association and is now in the possession of the Canadian War Museum.

Not only did the "Dak" carry men and supplies in great quantity, but it served as a glider tug during the airborne invasion of Europe. It was recognized as one of the most important tools available to the Allies. And it remained in military service throughout the Korean War and into the Vietnam conflict.

The first Daks to arrive in Canada were the 169 machines acquired by the RCAF between March 1943 and August 1946. Some of them were to remain on Canadian Armed Forces strength as late as 1989. Beginning in June 1946, Trans-Canada Air Lines replaced their Lockheed 14/18 fleet with three C-49s and 27 C-47s converted by Canadair to like-new DC-3s. Canadian Pacific, Maritime Central and other Canadian operators also added DC-3s to their fleets. But the first of the DC series to fly with Canadian registration was CF-BPP, a DC-2 introduced by Canadian Colonial Airlines in August of 1939. Many DC-3s are in museums including two in the National Aviation Museum, CF-TDF (one of TCA's original C-49s) and an ex-RCAF Dakota. Another DC-3 is flown by the Canadian Warplane Heritage in the markings of one of the 436 Squadron machines active in Burma and bearing the legend "Canucks Unlimited," the unit's unofficial name.

76.3 cm x 101.6 cm (30" x 40")
Canadian War Museum

Action at Schwebo – 1945
Robert W. Bradford (1923–   )

Year painted: 1972
Acrylic on canvas

Bristol Beaufighter

"Whispering Death"

With two large engines thrusting ahead of a minimal nose and cockpit, the Bristol Beaufighter, even at rest, had a purposeful appearance. Muscular agressiveness was its most striking characteristic. The "Beau" was fast, manoeuverable and, with four 20-mm cannon and six machine guns, more heavily armed than any comparable aircraft on either side. Equipped with rockets, it was said to be capable of delivering the equivalent of a cruiser's broadside.

Bristol's big fighter grew out of a need, perceived on the eve of war, for a two-seat heavy fighter with the range most easily obtained from a twin. Such an aircraft was best suited to the role of night fighter, and a light bomber, the Bristol Blenheim, was pressed into service. Although a world-beater in the mid-'30s, it was obsolescent by the outbreak of war and lacked the speed to cope with contemporary German bombers. Early in 1939, Bristol proposed fitting a new forward fuselage and considerably larger engines to their marginally successful Beaufort torpedo bomber. They obtained Air Ministry approval and built a prototype which flew scant months later in

July. With Bristol Hercules engines, its performance resulted in substantial orders and eventually more than 5,500 Beaufighters were built.

In service, the Beaufighter enjoyed immediate success as a night fighter, taking a toll of the German Dornier Do 17s and Junkers Ju 88s which had switched to night bombing during the winter months following the RAF victory in the Battle of Britain. While these fast, light bombers had been able to outrun the Blenheims that were their first opposition, they met more than their match in the Beaufighter, fitted as it was with the newly perfected Airborne Interception (A.I.) radar.

Once production gained momentum, Beaufighters were made available to Coastal Command for use as strike aircraft against submarines and shipping. Again they excelled. With their heavy firepower they could inflict mortal damage on surface craft and there are many reports of floating debris being all that remained of smaller ships once the smoke and spray from a Beaufighter attack had settled. Their rugged radial engines, armour, and sturdy construction enabled

them to absorb the considerable flack damage that was always a part of low-level strikes, and still return safely to base. As fighters, they ranged the Bay of Biscay and made it much safer for Allied ships and aircraft enroute to the Mediterranean. They also patrolled the North Sea and rendered the later stages of the approaches to England unsafe for German bombers and subs preying on Atlantic convoys. Beaufighters flew in North Africa, and in the far east the Japanese called them "Whispering Death" because their unusually quiet sleeve-valve engines allowed them to attack almost unheard.

In Bob Curry's oil painting, a pair of 252 Squadron RAF Coastal Command Beaufighters cruise over Brixham harbour. Bob has lovingly rendered their chipped and stained paint and the dented skin that soon came to characterize all operational fighting aircraft.

Four RCAF squadrons flew Beaufighters, 404 with Coastal Command and 400, 406 and 410 as night-fighter units. Many more Canadians served as crew on Beaus with other RAF units.

86.4 cm x 91.5 cm (32" x 36")
Collection of the artist

Guardian Angels – 1944
Robert Curry (1942–   )

Year painted: 1990
Oil on canvas

Avro Lancaster X
Unmatched Load Lifter

The Lancaster was unquestionably the best of the World War II night bombers, and its fame in the bombing role is challenged only by the Boeing B-17 Flying Fortress. While the "Lanc" did not boast the same weight in defensive armament nor fly as high as the B-17, it carried at least twice and occasionally better than three times the B-17's bomb-load. But comparisons are difficult: the Lanc flew at night while the Fortress operated in daylight in massed formations. Lancasters formed a large portion of the bomber streams that left wartime England nightly for targets in Germany and occupied Europe. For those below, in Britain and the occupied countries, the sound of their engines provided a continuing source of encouragement.

The immediate predecessor of the Lancaster was the twin-engined Manchester, first air-tested in July 1939. It was immediately pressed into squadron service, with unfortunate results due mainly to its unproven Rolls-Royce Vulture "X" engines. The Vultures seldom produced their rated 1,760 hp and were prone to failure, resulting in all-too-frequent forced landings behind enemy lines. It was apparent that the Manchester airframe/engine combination was not a happy one and that more power and greater reliability were sorely needed. The wing was re-designed with six-foot extensions on either side, and each Vulture replaced by a pair of Merlins. The fuselage with its 33-foot bomb bay, remained unchanged. But with better than 3,000 additional horsepower from its four Merlins, the new Manchester III, or Lancaster as it was renamed, became a superlative warplane.

The Avro bombers' exploits are legend. Lancasters were chosen to carry the drum-like bouncing bombs that shattered the Mohne and Eder dams. They dropped the first 8,000-lb bombs and then 12,000-lb deep-penetration "Tallboys" to collapse tunnels, crush submarine pens and eventually to sink the battleship *Tirpitz*. Only Lancs were capable of carrying Tallboys, and they were to do even better: modified, they could deliver the 22,000-lb "Grand Slam." Lancs equipped more than 60 squadrons including 14 RCAF units. In all, 7,366 Lancasters were built, 422 in Canada.

In Mike Martchenko's painting, the first of these, KB700, is shown on 6 August 1943, flying over the Victory Aircraft plant at Malton, near Toronto, where she was built. Christened the *"Ruhr Express,"* she flew a total of 85 missions with 405 and then 419 Squadrons before being written off in a landing accident. Two Lancasters are preserved in Canada, one in the NAM (KB944) and the other by the Canadian Warplane Heritage, dedicated to the memory of Andy Mynarski, who won the Victoria Cross on a 419 Squadron Lanc. Others exist in various Canadian locations as deteriorating outdoor memorials.

61.0 cm x 76.0 cm (24" x 30")
David Metcalfe, Aviation Art Canada

The Ruhr Express – 1943
Michael Martchenko (1942–   )

Year painted: 1988
Acrylic on board

de Havilland D.H. 98 Mosquito
Most Versatile of Warplanes

While the Mosquito is now recognized as one of the truly great aircraft of World War II, her manufacturers had found it extremely difficult even to obtain approval for the construction of a prototype. The concept of sacrificing a warplane's defensive armament totally, in the interest of speed, was completely foreign to current official thought. By combining the smallest possible airframe that could carry the necessary crew and bomb-load with the power of a medium bomber – and the tough but light all-wood construction which the firm had pioneered – de Havilland arrived at a very fast and manoeuverable aeroplane. Eliminated completely were the heavy turrets with their guns and ammunition and the additional crew needed to man them. The prototype flew initially on 25 November 1940 and revealed a level speed of close to 400 mph – and the agility of a fighter. The Air Ministry could not help being impressed, and the D.H. 98 was ordered into large-scale production.

The first variant to enter service was not a bomber but a photo-reconnaissance machine, which more than fulfilled the manufacturer's expectations, proving capable of easily outrunning Messerschmitt Bf 109s. With a 3,500-mile range, the PR "Mossie" was able to investigate the most remote corners of occupied Europe, challenged only by anti-aircraft fire or by the rare fighter positioned sufficiently high above the British aircraft to catch it in a dive.

Very soon, Mosquito bombers were also in squadron service, carrying 4,000-lb bomb-loads into Germany with equal impunity. Their range and speed enabled them to carry out raids with pin-point precision – on one occasion punching holes in the walls of Amiens prison, allowing condemned resistance fighters to escape. The Mosquito was proving to be the most aptly named of aircraft.

The Pathfinder units who marked targets for the night-bomber streams very soon adopted the Mosquito, which also flew diversionary raids with small numbers of aircraft dropping bombs and "chaff," the small strips of aluminum foil which could register on enemy radar as squadrons of phantom aircraft.

As a fighter, the Mosquito had its glazed nose replaced with a solid one containing a battery of four .30-cal guns and four 20-mm cannon. And again, the Mossie's role was over enemy territory, flying night 'intruder' missions which often involved visits to enemy night-fighter bases. There they would surreptitiously join the landing circuit to prey on aircraft returning from their forays against Allied bombers.

Robert Bradford has painted one such instance. This small and spontaneous painting was prepared as a study for a work that was never completed. A Mosquito from 418 Squadron flown by S/L Russ Bannock with F/L Bob Burns as his navigator/radar operator has managed to bring down a Junkers Ju 88 night fighter. In the last months of the war, Mossies ranged freely over Europe in daylight, attacking trains, road transport, river barges and other 'targets of opportunity'.

To supplement British production, plans were made to build Mosquitoes in Canada at de Havilland's Downsview plant, and the first example flew on 23 September 1942 with Ralph Spradbrow as pilot. Of a total Mosquito production of 7,781 machines, 1,033 were built in Canada, two-thirds of them as bombers. The Mossie's service-life lasted to 1953, but it continued on after that in civil use in the high-level aerial photo-survey role. A number of Mosquitoes have been preserved in museums around the world including one example in the National Aviation Museum. Another is being rebuilt in Vancouver by the Canadian Museum of Flight and Transportation.

30.5 cm x 45.7 cm (12" x 18")
Collection of the artist

Mosquito Intruder – 1944
Robert W. Bradford (1923–   )

Year painted: 1971
Oil on board

Possibly the Best World War II Fighter

The Mustang was one of the few aircraft in World War II that did not have pre-war origins. Early in 1940, the British Government Purchasing Mission placed an order with North American Aviation, manufacturer of the Harvard and Mitchell, for Curtiss P-40s. But, rather than build the aging Kittyhawk, the California firm offered to design a machine better suited to the demands of the air war in Europe, utilizing the latest in aerodynamics and construction methods. An agreement was signed in April and by late October, an amazingly short period, the prototype was ready for testing. The new NA-73 more than met expectations; with the same Allison engine as the P-40, it achieved a level speed of 390 mph. The RAF ordered it in quantity. United States Army Air Force interest kindled, and they ordered a ground-attack version, the A-36. But, with manoeuverability and speed to burn, the new machine's potential as a fighter

was obvious; it became the famed P-51.

In British service, the Mustang (the new fighter's RAF name) served in the fighter-reconnaissance role on Army Co-operation duties; lacking a supercharged engine, it performed best at lower altitudes. But, equipped with a battery of cameras, it excelled at obtaining vital photo intelligence. With four .50 and four .30 guns (or four 20-mm cannon), it could knock out ground targets and was more than a match for enemy fighters that might venture down to its preferred operating levels. Three RCAF squadrons – 400, 414 and 430 – flew Mustang Is and IIs.

In 1942, the RAF arranged for a Mustang to be experimentally fitted with a Merlin engine to improve performance at higher altitudes. As had been the case with the Lancaster, this second marriage was an impressive success. Eventually, Packard-built Merlins were standardized in Mustangs IIIs and IVs, arguably

the best piston-engined fighters of the war. Range, especially, was outstanding. Postwar, the Mustang served with RCAF regular and reserve units from 1947 until 1956. A Mustang IV (P-51D) is on display in the National Aviation Museum and another, owned by the Canadian Warplane Heritage of Hamilton, Ontario, performs regularly at airshows. Dozens more, including many ex-RCAF machines, are flown privately in the US and often make Canadian appearances.

Eric Aldwinckle, an official war artist with the RCAF, worked for a period with 430 Squadron. In the painting opposite, called *Invasion Pattern,* he has shown an RCAF Mustang flying over a Normandy beach on a solitary "recce" mission into France in June 1944, shortly after D-Day. The sand below is still cluttered with abandoned landing craft and is deeply rutted with tracks of the Allied tanks they brought ashore.

Invasion Pattern – 1944
Eric Aldwinckle (1909–1980)

Year painted: 1945
Oil on canvas

85.5 cm x 85.5 cm (34 1/2" x 34 1/2")
Canadian War Museum

Hawker Typhoon

Tank Buster Par Excellence

Few warplanes have so completely epitomized pugnacity and power as the mighty Typhoon, Hawker's successor to the Hurricane. Where the Spitfire's aesthetic perfection belied its deadliness, there was no mistaking the purpose for which the "Tiffie" had been designed. Its blunt spinner, huge underslung radiator and broad-shouldered stance all characterized a rugged heavyweight.

Although the Typhoon's Hurricane ancestry was discernable in her lines and her comparable size, she weighed almost twice as much. Her massive Napier Sabre 24-cylinder 'H' type engine contributed much of the weight but provided over 1,000 hp more than the Hurricane I's Merlin, and an almost 100 mph increase in speed. The Typhoon was in fact the first RAF aircraft to exceed 400 mph in level flight. In spite of this, when she was introduced operationally in mid-1941, she was not a success in her intended role as an interceptor; she experienced engine troubles, lost her performance edge at altitude and suffered occasional structural failures.

Happily, she was given the opportunity to demonstrate her low-level potential by chasing down the Focke Wulf Fw 190 "tip-and-run" bombers that attacked English targets in daylight and that were too fast for the contemporary variants of Spitfire. After D-Day, when the war moved across the English Channel into Normandy, the Typhoon came into her own as the best ground-attack aircraft the Allies possessed. Uncounted numbers of trains, tanks and other military vehicles were knocked out by low-flying Typhoons in close tactical support of the advancing Allied troops. Squadrons of "Tiffies" circled in "cab rank" above the advancing Allied armies. They were called down as needed, by a ground controller, to attack whatever targets were identified. RCAF squadrons 438, 439 and 440 flew the Typhoon, as did many Canadian pilots with RAF units. The Typhoon was armed with four 20-mm cannon, and carried either two 1,000-lb bombs or eight 60-lb rockets. In his lively acrylic, painted as a cover for the *Journal* of the Canadian Aviation Historical Society, Les Waller has shown a pair of Typhoons swooping through the smoke of a burning railway yard – a favoured target.

No Typhoons were ever seen in Canada, although a single Tempest (an immediate lineal descendant) was sent here for cold-weather trials, and the Royal Canadian Navy flew Hawker Sea Furies, last in the long line of Hawker piston-engined fighters. In Canada, Sea Furies are to be found in the NAM collection and in the Calgary Aerospace Museum. Others have been modified for air racing in the US. Of the more than 3,300 Typhoons built, only one remains extant, in the RAF Museum at Hendon near London, England.

30.5 cm x 40.6 cm (12" x 16")
Collection of the artist

Typhoon Sweep – 1944
Les Waller (1931–   )

Year painted: 1980
Acrylic on board

To Canadians, the Corsair will be forever associated with the memory of Lieutenant Robert Hampton ("Hammy") Gray, VC, DSC, Royal Canadian Navy Volunteer Reserve. He won the Victoria Cross for pressing home an attack in his damaged aircraft and sinking the Japanese escort vessel *Amakusa* in Onagawa Bay on the coast of Honshu Island on 9 August 1945. Gray lead a flight of Fleet Air Arm Corsairs from the British carrier HMS *Formidable*. Don Connolly brings the viewer tightly in behind Gray's aircraft as it closes with its target to a point where its bombs could not miss. Moments later, his aircraft rolled inverted, and crashed into the sea beyond the *Amakusa*.

One of the finest naval fighters of World War II, the Chance-Vought Corsair did not see service in its designed role as a carrier fighter until late 1944, although it had first flown in 1940 prior to the American entry into the war. In fact, Fleet Air Arm carriers of the Royal Navy operated the Corsair for the better part of a year before it was approved for use on US carriers. However, the "Whistling Death" (as it was dubbed by the Japanese) had long since proven its worth in combat. Since 1942, the US Marine Corps had flown it as a land-based fighter, from hastily carved island strips. The majority of that service's most successful pilots owed their effectiveness to the Corsair, and some naval units also did well with it from shore strips.

The Corsair was a big aircraft. It weighed seven tons loaded, and was the first US aircraft to be fitted with a 2,000 hp engine. It was also the first American machine to exceed 400 mph in level flight, just as the Hawker Typhoon had done with the RAF. The two types were also closely comparable in size, power and weight. Both machines could carry a 2,000-lb bomb-load and excelled in ground attack. However, the Corsair's air-cooled P&W Double Wasp was not as tempermental as the Typhoon's liquid-cooled Napier Sabre. The Typhoon did not perform as well at high altitude, although its successor, the Tempest, certainly did.

The bent or inverted gull-wing that characterized the Corsair was an unmistakable recognition feature. This unusual configuration, reminiscent of the German Junkers Ju 87 Stuka, had been chosen to provide ground clearance for the huge 13-foot, nine-inch prop, without using an unduly high – and fragile – undercarriage. But the Corsair did tend to bounce on landing and this propensity, coupled with the absence of any forward view over the long, blunt nose while in a landing attitude, resulted in its lengthy restriction to land-based operation – except by the Fleet Air Arm. Eventually, after the cockpit was raised and the undercarriage liveliness dampened, the Corsair was approved for use on US carriers and remained in service into the Korean War.

The only Corsair to be seen in Canada is an FG1D (Goodyear-built), flown by the Canadian Warplane Heritage in the markings of Lt. Robert Hampton ("Hammy") Gray, VC, DSC, RCNVR.

60.9 cm x 91.4 cm (24" x 36")
Canadian War Museum

Finale – 1945
Don Connolly (1931–   )

Year painted: 1988
Oil on canvas

Canadair/Lockheed CF-104s
Stephen Snider

Post-World War II

In August 1946, a Gloster Meteor twin-engined jet fighter was unloaded from a ship at Montreal and shipped to St Hubert Airport for assembly. This was the first jet aircraft to be seen in Canada. The pilots selected to fly it and a second machine were three RCAF/RAF veterans: F/L Bill McKenzie, F/L Jack Ritch and S/L Shan Badoux. McKenzie and Ritch had both flown Spitfires with 609 Squadron RAF and were among those chosen to become the first Allied service pilots to fly the revolutionary new aircraft. When Bill McKenzie was checked out on a Meteor at Farnborough, he became Canada's first jet pilot.

No. 609 Squadron operated Spitfire VIIIs and gradually converted to Meteors as they became available. To build public morale in the face of flying bomb (the infamous V-1 "buzz bomb") attacks on London, Winston Churchill had requested that Hitler's new terror weapon be countered by the RAF's own new, top-secret equipment. Germany's pulse-jet-powered "doodle bugs" were attacked as soon as they were spotted over the Channel by Mosquitoes, Mustangs, Tempests and Meteors in succession. The Meteors (whose existence had been a closely guarded secret), because of their marginally greater speed, were assigned the perilously narrow band just ahead of the barrage balloon and anti-aircraft defences of London. Their targets had to be located quickly and attacks initiated with speed and precise timing. The pilots of 609 did succeed in bringing down 19 of the diminutive flying robots, and it was a 609 pilot, "Dizzy" Dean, who first slipped his wing under the wing of a bomb and tipped it to explode harmlessly in a field. Widely reported, this stunt captured the imagination of the public. But repetition was not encouraged: the wing of Dean's Meteor had been so badly damaged that the aircraft had to be returned to the factory. Bill McKenzie did bring down a bomb with his guns, in the approved manner.

Following a spectacular demonstration before foreign air attachés at Ottawa, the two Canadian Meteors were flown at airshows all across the country, with Ritch and McKenzie as pilots. The artist, Les Waller, has captured Meteor FE 345 performing a roll at one such appearance. Both pilots found these first-generation jets with their quiet, vibration-free cockpits and lack of propeller torque easier and far more enjoyable to fly than the final-generation, piston-engined fighters that had preceded them.

33.0 cm x 35.5 cm (13" x 14")
Collection of the artist

The Gloster Meteor IV – 1946
Les Waller (1931–   )

Year painted: 1988
Acrylic on board

Canadair North Star

Adapted for Canadian Operations

Trans-Canada Air Lines had begun operations with the ten-seat Lockheed 10A and then upgraded to the bigger and faster Lockheed 14s and 18s, the latter carrying 18 passengers. These Lockheed aircraft saw not only TCA but Canadian Pacific Airlines through World War II. During the latter war years, TCA had flown the Atlantic regularly using modified Avro Lancasters. Their lean fuselages, which could carry an unmatched bomb-load, offered only cramped and noisy accommodation for a few VIP passengers. They would be completely unsatisfactory for an expanding civil operation. Looking forward to the post-war period, the Canadian government, who owned TCA, realized that a larger, longer-ranged aircraft would be needed, especially for trans-Atlantic routes. Canadair of Montreal was presented with the challenge of building such an aircraft.

The bulk of wartime Allied transport aircraft had been provided by US firms. Such military transports as the Douglas C-54 and Lockheed C-69 could readily be converted to their civil counterparts of DC-4 and Constellation, respectively. However, neither was pressurized and thus could not meet the high-altitude requirements of TCA. Canadair decided to rework the Douglas C-54 airframe, pressurizing the fuselage and adding a number of features from the larger and more modern DC-6. More power was needed, and TCA selected well-proven Rolls-Royce Merlins in place of the radials which powered the original aircraft.

The prototype, with registration CF-TEN-X, flew initially in July 1946, and the first production aircraft, one originally intended for the RCAF, was turned over to TCA in November of the same year. With 25 aircraft, the RCAF operated the largest North Star fleet. TCA received the first of 20 pressurized North Stars, CF-TFA, in October of 1947 and, for a number of years, "Canada's National Air Line" flew an aircraft comparable with any competitor, and better than most. The success of the North Star was not lost on other airlines; unfortunately, the licensing agreement with Douglas precluded sales other than in Canada and England. In 1949, British Overseas Airways Corporation, which was getting uneven service from their postwar derivatives of bombing aircraft, ordered a fleet of 22 to which they gave the type name Argonaut. Canadian Pacific Airlines purchased four, calling them Canadair Fours, and it is one of these, the *Empress of Vancouver*, that is elegantly depicted by Les Waller in its gleaming natural metal finish. This oil painting was commissioned originally for the book, *The Canadair North Star*, written by Larry Milberry.

North Stars and Argonauts represented a significant accomplishment by Canada's aircraft industry. Unfortunately, they are now best remembered for the noise of their Merlins as well as the glow and occasional flames from the inboard exhaust stacks only scant feet away from the forward passenger seats. To lessen the noise and eliminate an often unnerving night-time spectacle, TCA designed a system to collect the inboard exhaust and expel it unseen, on the opposite side of the engine. Although the problem was solved, no piston-engined airliner approached the smoothness and quiet of the succeeding generation of jets.

By 1961 the North Star was being replaced as first-line equipment by larger aircraft such as the Super Constellation (with TCA); however, many of them enjoyed extended careers with smaller airlines. None are flying today. An ex-RCAF North Star can be seen in the National Aviation Museum.

30.5 cm x 49 cm (12" x 19 ½")
Collection of the artist

Canadair Four, *Empress of Vancouver* – 1947
Les Waller (1931–   )

Year painted: 1982
Oil on canvas panel

de Havilland DHC-2 Beaver

A Rugged Customer

The Beaver was the second aircraft to be designed by DHC (de Havilland Aircraft of Canada); the first was the DHC-1 Chipmunk. All pre-war and wartime DHC production had been of aircraft designed by the parent firm in England. As the DHC-2, the Beaver was built to specifications evolved in consultation with pilots from the Ontario Department of Lands and Forests and other bush operators who recognized a need for a new utility transport of sturdy and easily maintained all-metal construction. A rugged and reliable engine was an obvious requirement. While the 330 hp de Havilland Gipsy Queen was initially considered, a more suitable air-cooled radial, the 450 hp Pratt & Whitney Wasp Junior, fortunately was found to be available in quantity (and brand new), as war surplus. Another asset was the high-lift wing, designed by DHC, with a new airfoil and ailerons co-ordinated to augment the flaps, for extra lift. This combination of abundant power and an efficient wing established DHC in the new field of short take-off and landing (STOL) aircraft, and the Beaver became the first of the highly successful series of machines that made de Havilland Canada world leaders in this branch of aviation.

The first flight of the Beaver occurred on 16 August 1947 with Russ Bannock (of Mosquito intruder fame) at the controls. The Beaver proved to be just as lively a performer as expected. The Ontario government, satisfied with the results of their collaboration with DHC, placed an order for 40 machines. These replaced the Stinson Reliants, Norsemans and other types that had made up their fleet. There was also a steady stream of orders from civil operators such as Fecteau Transport Aerienne and Pacific Western Airlines.

However the Beaver's reputation was greatly enhanced when, in 1949, it handily won a competition set up by the USAF and US Army for a liaison/utlity transport. Eventually, orders totalling 980 L-20s, as the Beaver was called in military service, were placed by the US government. The Beaver gave outstanding service during the war in Korea, where it earned the nickname the "Generals Jeep." All war-surplus Beavers to be sold in Canada were returned for conversion by DHC, and they amounted to a considerable number. In all, 1,573 Beavers were built and they have operated in 62 countries under all climatic conditions, peforming equally well on wheels, skis or floats. A single example was fitted with the larger Alvis Leonides engine in England, as the Beaver II. DHC developed the Turbo Beaver, powered with the Pratt & Whitney PT6, and a small number of these have been built. They are even better performers than their predecessors and have a larger cabin. However, the high initial cost of the engine has precluded their widespread use.

Although the design is over 40 years old, very few have found their way into museums and, of the half-dozen on exhibit around the world, most are in military collections. Beavers are still highly productive, working aircraft and, as such, are too valuable to be retired for display. Happily, the prototype (CF-FHB) was obtained by the National Aviation Museum after 35 years of service.

In Robert Bradford's painting, Beaver CF-GBD, operated by Eastern Provincial Airways, is seen at a remote lake in Newfoundland, picking up a party of geological surveyors under the leadership of Dr David Baird, OC. Dr Baird subsequently became the founding Director of the National Museum of Science and Technology (which included the National Aeronautical Collection) from 1966 to 1981. The painting was presented to Dr Baird upon his retirement.

50.0 cm x 65.0 cm (19 3/4" x 25 1/2")
Dr. David M. Baird

Beaver at Work – **1950s**
Robert W. Bradford (1923–)

Year painted: 1982
Acrylic on canvas

Avro C102 Jetliner

The First North American Jet Airliner

Although the cancellation of the Avro Arrow has been mourned with lasting passion, the failure of the Jetliner, when success seemed so close, has been accepted with resignation. The heady sense of pride which Canadians had in the Arrow, possibly the best of its kind in the world, is understandable. And yet the creation of the first passenger jet, the Avro C102, to fly on this continent represented a comparable achievement, and its demise possibly a greater loss. It, too, could have been a "world beater."

The Jetliner grew out of an agreement between Avro Canada and Trans-Canada Air Lines on a set of specifications for a turbine-powered airliner to carry at least 36 passengers. Power was to be suppied by a pair of early Rolls-Royce Avon engines, but four lower-powered RR Derwents had to be substituted. Since calculations suggested that the engine change would result in less of a payload and a shorter range, TCA withdrew their support.

The Jetliner, registered as CF-EJD-X, first flew on 10 August 1949 at Malton Airport, adjacent to the Avro Plant on the outskirts of Toronto. It was the second jet-powered airliner in the world to fly. (The British de Havilland D.H. 106 Comet had taken to the air for the first time on July 27. The Boeing 707 would not fly for a further five years, and the comparable Douglas DC-9 not until 1965.) As Don Rogers, who, with Jimmy Orrell, piloted the Jetliner on its historic first flight and on many subsequent occasions, has said, development of the C102 would have given Canada a DC-9-sized aircraft ten or more years before the Douglas transport made its appearance.

The first months of air trials and demonstration flights were a time of triumph and accomplishment. Speeds often close to 500 mph were the norm on flights between major Canadian and American cities at heights far above those frequented by piston-engined airliners of the day. Those who flew in the Jet-liner were impressed, and several American carriers expressed an interest, notably Howard Hughes's Trans World Airlines. Tentative plans to build the Jetliner in the US were even drawn up. But foreign sales were not helped by the continuing apathy of Canada's national airline. Were the design shortcomings perceived by TCA engineers too great to be overcome by changes in a production version? Or was TCA simply unwilling to pioneer in the civil use of pure jet transport? Emphatic arguments have been made for both positions. Because of growing Cold War tensions, the Canadian government demanded that Avro give complete priority to the development and production of the CF-100 all-weather interceptor, and official interest in the Jetliner evaporated.

In November 1956, the Jetliner was broken up, with only the nose (including the flight deck) saved. This sad reminder of an endeavour that held such great promise is now on display in the National Aviation Museum.

45.5 cm x 56.0 cm (18" x 22")
National Aviation Museum
Gift from Paperboard Industries

Avro Canada C102 Jetliner – 1949
Robert W. Bradford (1923–   )

Year painted: 1962
Acrylic on canvas

Avro CF-100 Canuck
Designed and Built in Canada

In 1945, in the early days of the Cold War, no available aircraft met RCAF needs for a two-place, all-weather interceptor with sufficient range to patrol the vast Canadian North. And, if such an aircraft could be designed and built in Canada, it would eliminate reliance on foreign manufacturers. Since thousands of aircraft had been produced in Canada during World War II, the capability was not lacking.

Avro Canada, still in the process of being formed, was entrusted with the project. Operating out of the former Victory Aircraft facilities at Malton on the outskirts of Toronto, Avro settled upon an attractively simple arrangement with twin jet engines in long nacelles fitted snuggly against an especially graceful fuselage. The wings were tapered with no sweep-back, and their shape was reflected in that of the tailplane. Overall it was one of the most pleasingly proportioned of the first-generation jets.

Two prototypes, fitted with British Rolls-Royce Avon engines, flew first in January of 1950 and were tested in Canada and briefly at Wright Field in the US. There, the CF-100 impressed American test pilots, particularly with its quick take-off and climb. With more powerful Canadian-designed-and-built Orenda engines, the CF-100 entered squadron service in 1952 giving the RCAF an aircraft with performance approached by few contemporaries. In 1951, the CF-100 became the first straight-winged pure jet to exceed the speed of sound, doing so in a dive. But it was an era of rapid improvement for all types of aircraft. Although the CF-100 remained in first-line operations for a decade, near the end its crews were having difficulty intercepting the latest commercial jet airliners. A sweptwing development was considered and even reached the mock-up stage. However, it was dropped in favour of Avro's mighty Arrow, seen as a successor that would more than re-establish the RCAF with the finest all-weather interceptor in the world. But in 1959, the Arrow was cancelled, and for a brief span, the RCAF relied upon unmanned Bomarc anti-aircraft missiles. In 1962, McDonnell F-101B Voodoos, obtained off-the-shelf from the USAF, replaced the CF-100s and the Bomarcs were also phased out.

The assigned name of "Canuck" seems rarely to have been used. In a half-decade of development the "CF" or "Clunk" (as it was called by those connected with it) progressed through five Marks, each with sub variants.

Those RCAF pilots who flew sweptwing Sabre day fighters knew the CF by the more derogatory term "Lead Sled." In their more nimble machines they enjoyed a performance edge – but at night or when the weather closed in, the sky belonged to the CF-100 crews. The RCAF eventually accepted 692 CF-100s, and a further 53 were sold to Belgium. They were used by four Canadian NATO squadrons in Europe and by nine units in Canada. Bases at Comox, BC; Cold Lake, Alberta; North Bay and Uplands in Ontario, as well as Bagotville, and St Hubert in Quebec formed a defensive chain across Canada. In Europe, Canadian squadrons flew out of Grostenquin and Marville in France and Zweibrucken and Baden-Soellingen in Germany. The armament of Marks up to the 4 consisted of eight .50-cal machine guns and wing-tip pods, each containing a cluster of 29 unguided rockets. The final Mark 5 carried only rockets.

In gleaming aluminum, Les Waller has shown one of the last CFs to remain operational, a machine loaned to Pratt & Whitney Canada for use as an engine test-bed.

33.0 cm x 45.7 cm (13" x 18")
Pratt & Whitney Canada

The Last CF-100 in Flight – 1983
Les Waller (1931–   )

Year painted: 1983
Acrylic on board

Canadair/North American F-86 Sabre
Best in its Class

Having produced the superlative Mustang, North American Aviation were in the forefront of World War II fighter design, and their reputation was to be further enhanced by the postwar Sabre. Yet the F-86 evolved from North American's first jet design, a rather portly, straight-winged naval fighter, the FJ-1 Fury. Only a handful were built and a land-based version, the experimental XP-86, was rejected by the USAF. By this time, fortunately, the manufacturer had gained access to German wartime research and set about a drastic design revision. They swept the wings and tailplane back 35 degrees and fitted them to a much slimmer fuselage. Thus, the Sabre was born; mediocrity gave way to excellence.

Squadron Leader Andy Mackenzie ranked the Sabre with the Spitfire as his favourite aircraft. A World War II Spitfire ace, Mackenzie flew the Sabre with the RCAF and on exchange with the USAF in Korea. The finest F-86 variant was the Canadair-built Mark 6, fitted with the Canadian-designed Orenda engine of 7,275 pounds thrust.

For a pilot, the Sabre was an ideal mount. He sat high and well forward under a large bubble canopy with a fine field of vision, far better than that of any World War II piston-engined fighter. But of greater importance was the fact that the Sabre offered a performance matched only by one other aircraft of its day, the Russian MiG-15, which preceded it into the air by a scant three months.

During the Korean War, the Chinese Air Force MiGs that suddenly appeared in support of retreating North Korean troops outclassed the World War II piston-engined fighters and first-generation jets used by UN forces assisting the South Koreans. Since only one western aircraft could match the MiG-15, the training of units newly equipped with the Sabre was hastened – and completed in Korea. The Sabre immediately established an ascendancy over its smaller and slightly more powerful rival. Pilot experience and training resulted in a lop-sided victory ratio.

When the RCAF squadrons serving at NATO bases in England, Germany and France initiallly received their Canadair Sabres in 1951, they were the first NATO units to operate sweptwing fighters. Canadian pilots referred affectionately to the Sabre as the "Sword" and seldom used its assigned name.

The aircraft dramatically painted by Peter Mossman, gleaming in sunlight above the clouds, is a Mark 5 (RCAF 23154) belonging to 416 Lynx (City of Oshawa) Squadron. The painting was created as cover art for the CAHS *Journal.* It is owned by Ken ("Haggus") Hagarty, a former F-86 pilot who made nine trans-Atlantic flights with 416 Squadron and the Overseas Ferry Unit (OFU), delivering Sabres to Europe.

All told, 12 RCAF–NATO squadrons and six auxiliary squadrons flew Sabres, operating them until 1963. The Sabre years are remembered with nostalgia as a golden era, when the RCAF boasted many of the world's best pilots flying the première fighter aircraft. They won international competitions with regularity. Those who saw the strikingly painted RCAF Sabre aerobatic team of the '50s, the Golden Hawks, will not forget their exuberant airshow performances.

Canadair built over 1,800 Sabres in six variants, not only for the RCAF, but for the RAF (their first sweptwing operational fighter), and the air forces of Colombia, Germany and Turkey. Famed American pilot Jacqueline Cochrane used a Canadair Sabre to set three air-speed records for women. A number of Sabres have been preserved, mostly on pedestals as civic monuments or CF base "gate guardians." Two Mark 6s are displayed at the National Aviation Museum, one in the overseas livery (camouflage) of 444 Squadron and the other as a Golden Hawk.

Year painted: 1986
Acrylic on board

Lynx on the Prowl – **1955**
Peter Mossman (1936–)

51.0 cm x 61.0 cm (20" x 24")
Kenneth Hagarty

Avro CF-105 Arrow
Canada's Most Famous Aircraft

Is there a Canadian today, apart from the most youthful, who is not familiar with the saga of the Avro Arrow – more than 30 years after its demise? It has been the subject of a half-dozen books, innumerable articles, documentary films and even a theatrical production. Yet, only five Arrows were ever built, while as many more had reached varying stages of completion. They made a total of 66 flights totalling 70 and one-half flying hours while still months away from operational service. But the aircraft caught the imagination of the Canadian public. Promising a performance – possibly unmatched, and certainly unexcelled – by any foreign contemporary, the Arrow became a symbol of Canadian excellence and a source of national pride. Its cancellation on "Black Friday," 20 February 1959, shocked the country. All employees were sent home, save for the handful needed to carry out an order to break up the five aircraft. Their destruction has often been called malicious, and, in the words of Pierre Berton, "unmitigated vandalism." This action probably resulted in the subsequent defeat of the Conservative government lead by John Diefenbaker.

The Arrow was a big, sophisticated, shoulder-wing delta. In its operational Marks, it would have been capable of Mach 2.5 – 2,000 mph, powered with two Canadian-designed Iroquois engines, each ultimately of 21,000 lb of thrust. They would enable the Arrow to operate at altitudes aproaching 70,000 feet and provide a range of more than 1,000 miles. The aircraft weighed 30 tons loaded (only a few tons less than the Lancaster) and, unlike most contemporary fighters, carried all of its armament internally. The Iroquois-powered version was about to be tested at the time of cancellation, but the earlier versions, with lower-powered American Pratt & Whitney J-75 engines had met every expectation handsomely. The Arrow was conceived in an age when speed was paramount, and its performance in the years since has scarcely been bettered. If anything, its modern counterparts are not as fast; manoeuverability has become a priority and the newer machines are more flexible in their capabilities.

The five Arrows were flown by only four pilots: Jan "Zura" Zurakowski (chief test pilot), W. "Spud" Potocki, Peter Cope and F/L Jack Woodman (RCAF test pilot). Only Potocki flew all five aircraft, amassing almost half of the Arrows' total flying time.

The angular, yet extremely graceful Arrow – it was one of the most attractive of delta designs – is not an easy painting assignment, with its white, anti-flash paint and bright red day-glo extremities. Among the many attempts, one of the most successful is Steve Snider's depiction of an imaginary situation, with Arrow 202 rolling to port and 203 probably about to follow. (In reality there were never two Arrows in the air simultaneously.) One is tempted to visualize the Arrow in the camouflage colour schemes it might have worn had it become operational.

With the Arrow gone, the RCAF were given the Bomarc anti-aircraft missiles. When they proved inadequate for continental defence, they were supplemented by McDonnell F-101B Voodoos (called CF-101s) from the USAF. The Bomarcs were soon retired – but the Voodoo performed well for more than two decades.

All that remains today of the Arrow, apart from photographs, film, and technical material hurriedly spirited away by employees, is a nose section from aft of the cockpit, a pair of wing tips and part of the undercarriage. These sad relics are to be seen in the National Aviation Museum.

58.5 cm x 78.7 cm (23" x 31")
Linda and Robert Ewles, Amorak Publishing

A Pair of Arrows – 1959
Steve Snider (1953–   )

Year painted: 1986
Acrylic on board

McDonnell CF-101 Voodoo

A Mighty Defender

The adjective "mighty" is often – and aptly – used to describe the Voodoo, which replaced the CF-100 in the all-weather interceptor role with the RCAF and CAF. The Voodoo was 13 feet longer than its predecessor, more than ten tons heavier and over twice as fast. It was, in fact, "red-lined" at the same permissable top speed as its successor, the CF-18 Hornet. At more than 25 tons, its weight easily doubled that of such World War II counterparts as the Mosquito and Beaufighter. By any standards it was an impressive aeroplane.

Although the Voodoo entered squadron service with the RCAF in 1962, the design began life in 1948 as the experimental XF-88 long-range escort fighter. During the Korean War, the concept was revived in a much scaled-up version as the F-101A, which flew initially in 1954. The two-seat F-101B interceptor followed in 1955, and it was this version that was selected by the RCAF to join the Bomarc anti-aircraft missile as a replacement for the cancelled Avro Arrow. (There was still a grave threat from manned Russian bombers.) The Bomarc was soon scrapped, but the Voodoo proved a fortunate choice. Re-designated as the CF-101, it remained in Canadian service for more than two decades.

The original 66 Voodoos obtained by the RCAF eventually equipped five squadrons operating out of four principal Canadian locations: Comox, British Columbia (409); Namao, Alberta (414); Bagotville, Quebec (425); and Chatham, New Brunswick (416); as well as from Uplands, Ontario (410) for a brief period. From these bases they ranged across the breadth of Canada, protecting the continent from aerial attack, electronically directed from NORAD headquarters in Colorado. With its speed and endurance, the Voodoo was capable of intercepting and destroying any manned bomber of its era. A typical mission might involve a two-hour flight of over 1,000 miles. The big McDonnell fighter carried sophisticated radar and was armed with both heat-seeking and radar-guided missiles to overcome whatever counter-measures an enemy might adopt. Machine guns were not thought necessary. Although Canadian Voodoos were never called upon to use their weapons "in anger," their crews were among the best trained and most efficient that any air force possessed.

The Voodoo, like the Starfighter, was a product of a time when speed was paramount among fighter requirements. Their successors are no faster. But more efficient engines now make for greater range, and computer-assisted flying affords a far more flexible mix of speed and manoeuverability. (Bob Merrick, a former Voodoo navigator, jokingly remarked that a Voodoo required two States in which to complete a turn. The Hornet can accomplish one within the confines of an airfield.) The Voodoo was an impressive performer, epitomizing sheer power, and was never more impressive than when its afterburners were used for a very quick climb to altitude.

In Graham Wragg's vigorous rendering, a pair of 416 (Lynx) Squadron Voodoos from CFB Chatham, are trailing a Soviet Tupolev Tu-50 'Bear D' turbo-prop reconnaissance/bomber that has intruded into Canadian air space. Such incursions once occurred regularly, made by aircraft following the polar route from Russia to Cuba. Invariably they were intercepted by Voodoos. The incident depicted was described to the artist by a Voodoo pilot. A numer of Voodoos have been preserved, some in museums such as the NAM and WCAM, and others as station "gate guardians."

51.0 cm x 63.5 cm (20" x 25")
Collection of the artist

The Lynx and the Bear – 1966
Graham Wragg (1943–   )

Year painted: 1981
Gouache on board

Canadair/Lockheed CF-104 Starfighter

The Missile with a Man in It

When the RCAF required a replacement for the superlative but aging F-86 Sabre, they chose the Lockheed Starfighter. Lockheed's machine had grown out of a need, made apparent by the Korean War, for an air-superiority fighter with greater speed, a higher ceiling and good manoeuverability. Speed and climb, the 104 possessed in abundance; the term "missile with a man in it" has been applied to several aircraft but to none more aptly than the Starfighter, with its wing span of less than 22 feet (and a wing area comparable to that of a light plane). Although the Starfighter was an impressive 55 feet in length, it was a small fighter for its era. Manoeuverability had been sacrificed for speed and it became the first mach 2-plus operational fighter. And yet, in terms of airframe arrangement, it bore a fleeting resemblance to the elderly T-33 Silver Star, a lineal ancestor and, for many years, the RCAF's principal jet trainer.

While only a handful of F-104As were built, they earned recognition disproportionate to their numbers – by breaking world records. In May 1958, a Starfighter was flown to a new altitude record of 91,243 feet, exceeding the previous record by two vertical miles. Later in the month, a Starfighter set an air-speed record of 1,404.9 mph, adding 200 mph to the previous record. The next year, the 104 became the first aircraft to exceed 30,000 metres (98,446 feet) by zooming to an altitude of 103,389 feet. In the process, all climb-to-altitude records were also broken.

Convinced that there was a market for such an outstanding performer, Lockheed proposed a slightly enlarged version for the West German Air Force, to replace their Sabres. The new machine promised to be equally well suited to Canada's strike/photo reconnaissance role in NATO. Strengthened for low-level operation, it was able to punch through turbulence which would have caused control problems for other fighters – and still provide a steady camera mount. As the F-104G, it became the most important and numerous variant of the Starfighter – some 2,500 being built, mostly outside of the US (in nine countries) under licence. Canadair of Montreal turned out 238 CF-104s, as they were designated in Canada, for the RCAF.

The first RCAF 104 was delivered to the RCAF station at Zweibrucken on 18 October 1962; they were eventually to equip eight squadrons, six strike and two 'recce'. Tom Bjarnason's dramatic painting shows a CF-104 at Baden-Soellingen in West Germany, about to move out from its dispersal area for a night sortie. The medium – coloured inks and white acrylic – is unusual and although difficult is used with spontaneity.

The CF-104 was not a forgiving aircraft and had to be flown by experienced pilots. However, despite its largely undeserved reputation as a "widow-maker," it was well liked and remained in first-line operation for over 20 years, until replaced by the CF-18 Hornet, starting in 1982. CF-104s continued flying with the CAF as late as 1988. While some Starfighters have been mounted on pedestals at CAF bases, an example is to be found in the NAM, not of an F-104G but of an earlier American-built 104A used on a successful Canadian-altitude-record attempt, attaining 100,110 feet in 1967. A CF-104 has recently been donated to the WCAM in Winnipeg.

46.7 cm x 68 cm (18 1/2" x 27")
Canadian War Museum

CF-104 in Dispersal: Baden-Soellingen – 1970
Tom Bjarnason (1925–)

Year painted: 1970
Coloured ink and acrylic on board

McDonnell Douglas CF-18 Hornet
Superlatively Versatile Fighter

With the CF-18 Hornet, the CAF was able to replace two quite different types of aircraft. By the late '70s, it was apparent that a successor would soon be needed for both the Canadair/Lockheed CF-104 Starfighters (used by the CAF's NATO squadrons in Germany) and the McDonnell CF-101 Voodoos (flown in Canada as all-weather long-range interceptors in fulfillment of our NORAD commitment). Both had enjoyed two decades of service. It was also intended that Hornets should replace the Canadair/Northrop CF-5 Freedom Fighters used by the RCAF in Europe and in Canada. In the event, the latter aircraft, a fine light-weight fighter, was retained and converted for the training role.

The CF-18 began life in 1974 as the somewhat smaller Northrop YF-17 Cobra competing to fill a requirement for a USAF lightweight fighter. When their contender was beaten out by the General Dynamics F-16 Fighting Falcon, Northrop teamed up with McDonnell Douglas (as senior partner) to enlarge and strengthen the design and increase power to meet a US Navy requirement for a high-performance carrier fighter. This time they were successful, and the F/A-18, as it was redesignated, was ordered in quantity for both the USN and the Marine Corps.

Before the CAF settled upon the Hornet, they looked closely at several other choices; they then narrowed the list to the single-engined F-16, the Panavia Toronado (built jointly by England, Germany and Italy) and the F-18. The latter pair, both with twin-engines, were regarded as offering a safety edge for all-weather flying, although fewer aircraft could be obtained for the sum of money which the Canadian government felt it could afford. Eventually the Hornet won the contest. Similarly, it was chosen to re-equip the air forces of Australia and Spain.

For $5.2 billion, Canada would receive 138 Hornets beginning in 1982 – all but 40 being single-seat versions. Eventually they equipped eight squadrons. The Hornet is as fast as its Voodoo predecessor, but slower than the Starfighter, which it also replaced. However it is infinitely more manoeuverable than either of the earlier machines and far more of a 'pilot's aircraft'. It is fitted with a HUD (Head-Up Display) and HOTAS (Hands On Throttle And Stick) systems, which are complementary. The former projects all information onto the pilot's windscreen, while the latter places the selection of such information at his fingertips, without the need to release either stick or throttle – the most critical controls. The pilot can thus devote his attention entirely to what is happening outside of his aircraft. The only problem is with the assimilation and analysis of data – which must be done rapidly. But this has been a challenge which pilots have willingly accepted.

The Hornet can be used in both air-to-air and ground attack roles, but with different weapons. For the former, radar-guided Sparrow and heat-seaking Sidewinder missiles are used as well as a 20-mm cannon. For the latter, the missiles are replaced with bombs; more than eight tons of ordnance can be carried. During the Persian Gulf war, Canadian Hornets flew effectively in both modes.

Hornets are operated around the clock, and in this pastel painting, Tom Bjarnason has captured the floodlit drama of aircraft kept in constant readiness; the backlit Hornet has just returned from a flight. The locale is CFB Cold Lake, Alberta. The medium has been used thinly rather than in the heavy traditional manner, with carefully placed highlights of acrylic.

50.84 cm x 76.2 cm (20" x 30")
Canadian War Museum

Hornet at Readiness: Night – 1984
Tom Bjarnason (1925–   )

Year painted: 1984
Pastel on board

de Havilland Dash 8
Most Elegant of Small Airliners

The de Havilland Canada (a division of Bombardier) Dash 8 (DHC-8) is one the most attractive of current turboprop commuter aircraft. The sleek 'feeder-liner' grew out of the need for a short-haul transport in the 30-40-seat range, to fit between the Twin Otter (seating 24) and the 46-seat Dash 7. The Twin Otter, designed to meet a military requirement that did not materialize, had proven unexpectedly successful in the rapidly expanding commuter airline field in the US, as to a lesser degree had its much bigger brother, the Dash 7. These two machines firmly established de Havilland in the new field. The four-engined Dash 7, designed expressly for short-haul operation, epitomizes the advantages of STOL (short take-off and landing) capability. It can be aloft in an amazingly short distance – and climb steeply and almost noiselessly. When the Thames STOL Port in London, England, was first opened, the Dash 7 was the only aircraft approved for operation. In mountainous regions it is ideal, with a performance unmatched by any other fixed-wing civil transport of comparable size. Unforseen circumstances involving both economics and American politics combined, unfortunately, to deprive it of the success that had at first seemed imminent.

At the same time, design and construction of the Dash 8 was getting underway. A de Havilland team had toured the US, visiting small airlines and collecting data on their aircraft requirements, and it was to these specifications that DHC built the Dash 8. The one criticism leveled at the Dash 7 was that it lacked speed. This could not be said of the elegant Dash 8 with its two PW120 turboprops delivering a total of 4,000 hp. If the Dash 8 nose profile has a familiar look, reminiscent of Canadair's Challenger business jet, it is with good reason. Canadair made the Challenger loft-lines available to the Toronto firm. It first flew on 20 June 1983, officially.

Actually it had been airbourne somewhat earlier, during high-speed taxiing trials, with chief test pilot Bob Fowler at the controls. In spite of a world-wide depression, the Dash 8 has lived up to its promise and is gaining popularity with airlines. A substantial number are on order or have been delivered.

Robert Bradford's painting of the prototype Dash 8 with its strikingly simple colour scheme was created before the complete aircraft actually existed. There were no air-to-air photographs to provide inspiration and solve drawing problems. Bradford worked from technical drawings, from a few components on the line, from the wooden mockup and from a rather basic wind-tunnel model. That he produced such a dramatic painting is testimony to his ability. He later learned that photographs taken by the company very nearly duplicated his dramatic composition.

68 cm x 88.8 cm (27" x 35")
de Havilland

de Havilland Dash 8 – 1982
Robert W. Bradford (1923–   )

Year painted: 1981
Acrylic on canvas

D.H. 60X Cirrus Moth
Frank Taylor

Registrations and Designations

The letters and numbers that are associated with aeroplanes can bewilder the reader. A complete explanation might easily fill a book; what follows is an introduction. There are registrations (assigned by governments) and there are designations (given by manufacturers and by air services) to distinguish different types of aircraft. Here and in the individual entries, registrations are shown in small caps; designations are shown in full caps.

Registrations

Those prominent, five-letter groupings on the sides and wings of older aeroplanes are registrations, government-assigned, identification letters – much like automobile licence plates. These letters distinguish individual civil aircraft. First applied in 1920, they are still in use, less conspicuously, today.

Prior to World War I, aeroplanes were not licensed in any way and they were marked only at the whim of their owners. Not only were these aircraft few in number, their range and carrying capacity were negligible; governments saw little need to keep track of them.

However, World War I stimulated progress in aircraft design and performance. Almost overnight, the aeroplane became a viable means of rapid transport for both passengers and cargo. Following the Armistice in November 1918, large numbers of military aircraft were sold to civilian buyers who hastily pressed them into service all around the world. Sometimes the new owners modified them for passenger accommodation; more often, nothing was done beyond the removal of armament. In many instances, they still bore their wartime colour schemes and military markings. Thousands of airmen, released from the various air services, provided a ready supply of pilots eager to continue flying.

In the interests of safety particularly, government controls on flying became an obvious necessity. At the Paris Peace Conference of 1919, the delegates struck a sub-committee to deal with the international regulation of civil flying. This sub-committee formulated guidelines for licensing civil aircraft, worldwide, with individual registrations – national markings – for all machines.

The countries of the British Commonwealth were assigned the letter 'G' – to be used as a prefix, followed by a dash and four letters. Canadian aircraft would use CA as the initial two letters of this latter group. Accordingly, the first machine to receive a Canadian registration was a JN-4(Can), owned by the Aerial Service Company of Regina, Saskatchewan, which became G-CAAA. The next aircraft, G-CAAB, was another prairie-based JN-4. The first British civil aircraft to be marked was G-EAAA, and the first Australian, G-AUAA. French aircraft were assigned the 'F' prefix, Italy the 'I', and Germany, 'D'. The USA was allocated 'N', to be followed by a combination of numerals and occasional letters – the committee rightly anticipated that civil flying in

the States would be on a much greater scale than in other countries

The Canadian regulatory body, the Air Board, decided that military aircraft should also carry letter registrations, beginning with G-CY. Thus, an Avro 504K became G-CYAA. Initially, registrations were applied in full, within white panels painted over wartime colour schemes. As aircraft were refinished, their registrations were shortened to the last two letters, since the first three remained constant. (Although the same was true of privately owned aircraft, similar abbreviations were not permitted.) In 1928, a system of numerical registrations (or serials) replaced letter combinations on Canadian military aircraft and, in modified form, is still in use today.

Also in 1928, national markings were revised and Canadian aircraft began carrying the familiar CF- markings beginning with CF-AAA, assigned to a de Havilland Gipsy Moth. (British aeroplanes carried markings beginning G-A, which are still in use.) By the mid-'70s, the CF- series was becoming exhausted, in spite of the re-use of markings from aeroplanes that had been struck off the register because they were sold abroad, destroyed, or simply "reduced to produce." The new block that was opened began with C-G, reminiscent of the G-C series of a half-century

earlier. As well, a ruling required that CF- registrations be altered to read C-F whenever an aircraft was repainted. Happily, this rule has been relaxed to allow very old or historic aeroplanes to retain the dash in its original location.

Regulations also dictated the size of registration letters relative to the aircraft carrying them. When aeroplanes were not the common sight they are today, registrations were large and they provided each aircraft with an identity. Sometimes the letter combinations resulted in easily remembered, but charmingly nonsensical little words. For instance, G-CASK, a Fokker Super Universal illustrated in this book, was sometimes called "CASK" or simply "SK". A Vickers Viking IV, G-CAEB, was fondly referred to as "Old EB." And in 1946, "BUM" (a war-surplus Tiger Moth, CF-BUM) was to be seen at Toronto's Barker Field.

During World War II, RCAF and RAF aircraft were identified by small individual serial numbers applied on the rear fuselage, and by large 'designator' letters for squadron and individual aircraft. The DN carried by the Spitfires in Don Anderson's painting indicates that they were from 416 Squadron. The single letter (X on the foremost Spitfire) behind the roundel, identifies the particular aircraft. If DN-X was lost or transferred to another unit, the markings would be applied to a new machine.

Designations

From the time of the Wright brothers, as soon as an aircraft manufacturer produced a second, "improved" model, he faced the need to distinguish it from his earlier machine. Since each builder evolved his own system, the variety is vast, and will only be treated here as it applies to the aircraft that are illustrated and described in this book.

Fortunately, most aircraft types, whether Canadian, British or American, have been given names. Few Canadians have not heard of the *Silver Dart*, the Spitfire, or the Lancaster. But then there are the designations – the combinations of letters, numerals and punctuation – by which many aircraft, particularly American, are also identified. And these can be confusing. Military aircraft may bear both manufacturer's and service designations. The most famous Allied single-engined advanced trainer during World War II – illustrated by Tom Bjarnason – was called the NA-76 by her manufacturer (North American Aviation), the SNJ by the US Navy, the T-6 or Texan by the US Army Air Force, and the Harvard by the RAF and RCAF.

The American military system, first used by the US Army Air Service and continued by its successors, with prefixes denoting an aircraft's role followed by a dash and a number,

is well known. The "P" in P-51, for instance, stood for Pursuit, later giving way to "F" for Fighter. The US navy scheme was more complicated, with codes for the manufacturer, the aircraft's role, and the variant. The Canadian Warplane Heritage's Chance-Vought Corsair is an FG1D, meaning that it is the "D" model of the first ("1") naval fighter built by Goodyear ("G") under licence from Chance-Vought. The same aircraft, built by the designing firm, would be an F4U-1 with the "U" indicating Chance-Vought, and the "4" that it was their fourth naval fighter design. In British service the FG1D became, simply, the Corsair IV.

Happily, the USN has since adopted a system similar to the US Air Force. The Canadian Forces' McDonnell Douglas F-18 Hornet, although designed as a naval fighter, would bear the same designation (or possibly F/A-18, denoting its "Attack" as well as Fighter capability), even if used by the USAF.

When comparing American and British systems, one becomes aware of the US partiality for dashes (as in Curtiss JN-4, Douglas DC-3, and North American F-86) and the corresponding British use of periods (the Sopwith 2 F.1 and the de Havilland D.H. 98). When the US government decided to build the British de Havilland D.H. 4 under licence during World War I, it became the DH-4.

De Havilland in England designated all of their products successively with D.H., as with the D.H. 9A and the D.H. 80 Puss Moth. Their Canadian plant followed this practice with the aircraft that they built and assembled until the end of World War II. They then switched to the American style of designation for the postwar machines built to their own designs, beginning with DHC-1 for their Chipmunk trainer and continuing on through the DHC-8, the Dash 8 commuter liner.

Canadair followed a similar practice with their Tutor jet trainer, calling it the CL-41. The F-86 Sabre, built under licence, bore Canadair's factory designation CL-13. Avro Canada used neither dashes nor periods in their nomenclature, with the Canuck being the CF100 (the dash in CF-100 was added by the RCAF). Their Jetliner was the C102 and the Arrow, the CF105.

Fairchild Aircraft of Longueuil, Quebec, had names for only two of their models, the unsuccessful Sekani and their final design, the Husky. All of the others were known by designations only: the FC-2, the FC-2W-2, the 51, the 71, and the 82. The Super 71 and Super 71P had feet in both camps.

British manufacturers have always identified successive variants of the same aircraft as Marks, such as the Gloster Meteor Mark IV or,

simply, the Spitfire IX. Differences between Marks are recognized by the addition of a capital letter suffix – the Hawker Typhoon IB. American nomenclature recognizes variants by adding suffix letters, as with the North American P-51B, which in the RAF and RCAF was the Mustang III. The RCAF and CAF follow the British practice and distinguish variants by Marks. For instance the Canadair (North American) F-86E became the Sabre 6 (Mark 6 or Mk 6), with Arabic rather than Roman numerals.

Canada's Aviation Museums

*Where many of the historic aircraft mentioned
in this book may be seen*

Aerospace Museum of Calgary
64 McTavish Place NE, Calgary, Alberta.

Alberta Aviation Museum Association
*Building No.1, 11760 - 109 Street, Edmonton,
Alberta.*

Atlantic Canada Aviation Museum
*Near the Halifax International Airport, 1658
Bedford Highway, Bedford, Nova Scotia.*

Billy Bishop Heritage
*(contains no aircraft but many artifacts)
Owen Sound, Ontario*

British Columbia Aviation Museum
*3-3539 Norseman Road, Patricia Bay Airport,
Sidney, British Columbia.*

Brome County Historical Society
Paul Holland Museum, Knowlton, Quebec.

Canadian Museum of Flight and Transportation
*13527 Crescent Road, Surrey, British
Columbia.*

Canadian War Museum
1330 Sussex Drive, Ottawa, Ontario

Canadian Warplane Heritage Museum
*At Mount Hope Airport, near Hamilton,
Ontario.*

Collingwood Classic Aircraft Foundation
*Five miles south of Collingwood, Ontario, at
Collingwood Airport.*

Commonwealth Air Training Plan Museum
*On #10 Highway, one mile north of Trans-
Canada Highway, near Brandon, Manitoba.*

National Aviation Museum
*On Aviation Parkway at Rockcliffe Airport,
Ottawa, Ontario.*

Reynolds Aviation Museum
4110 - 57 Street, Wetaskiwin, Alberta.

Shearwater Aviation Museum
*Canadian Forces Base, Shearwater, Nova
Scotia*

Western Canada Aviation Museum
*Hangar T-2, 958 Ferry Road, Winnipeg,
Manitoba.*

Western Development Museum
*2935 Melville Street, Saskatoon,
Saskatchewan.*

World War I Flying Museum
*RR #1, Erin, Ontario, Billy Bishop hangar at
Brampton Airport.*

Index of Pilots

Suggested Reading

BAGLOW, Bob. *Canucks Unlimited: RCAF CF-100 Squadrons and Aircraft, 1952-1963*. Ottawa: Canuck Publications, 1985.

BALLANTINE, Ian, ed. *The Aviation Art of Keith Ferris*. New York: Peacock Press/Bantam Books, 1978.

CONNOLLY, Don. *Painting Planes: The Aviation Art of Don Connolly*. Stittsville, Ontario: Canada's Wings, 1982.

ELLIS, Frank H., and Ellis, Elsie E. *Atlantic Air Conquest*. Toronto: Ryerson Press, 1963.

ELLIS, Frank H. *Canada's Flying Heritage*. Toronto: University of Toronto Press, 1954.

ELLIS, John R. *The Canadian Civil Aircraft Register, 1920-1928*. Toronto: Canadian Aviation Historical Society, 1975.

ELLIS, John R. *The Canadian Civil Aircraft Register, 1929-1945*. Toronto: Canadian Aviation Historical Society, 1969.

FLOYD, Jim. *The Avro Canada C102 Jetliner*. Erin, Ontario: Boston Mills Press, 1986.

FULLER, G. A., Griffin, J. A., and Molson, K. M. *125 Years of Canadian Aeronautics: A Chronology 1840-1965*. Toronto: Canadian Aviation Historical Society, 1983.

GREEN, William, and Cross, Roy. *Jet Aircraft of the World*. London: Macdonald, 1955.

GREEN, William. *Famous Bombers of the Second World War*. London: Macdonald, 1959.

GREEN, Willam. *Famous Fighters of the Second World War*. London: Macdonald, 1957.

GRIFFIN, John. *Canadian Military Aircraft: Serials and Photographs*. Ottawa: The Canadian War Museum, 1969.

GUNSTON, Bill. *Aircraft of World War II*. London: Octopus Books, 1980.

GUNSTON, Bill. *Modern Military Aircraft*. London: Salamander Books, 1977.

HOTSON, Fred. *The de Havilland Canada Story*. Toronto: Canav Books, 1977.

JACKSON, A. J. *De Havilland Aircraft Since 1915*. London: Putnam, 1962.

KOSTENUCK, Samuel, and Griffin, John. *RCAF Squadrons and Aircraft*. Ottawa: The Canadian War Museum, 1977.

LARKIN, David, ed. *The Aviation Art of Frank Wootton*. New York: Peacock Press/Bantam Books, 1976.

MILBERRY, Larry. *Aviation in Canada*. Toronto: McGraw-Hill, 1979.

MILBERRY, Larry. *The Avro CF-100*. Toronto: Canav Books, 1981.

MILBERRY, Larry. *The Canadair North Star*. Toronto: Canav Books, 1982.

MILBERRY, Larry. *Canada's Air Force Today*. Toronto: Canav Books, 1987.

MILBERRY, Larry. *Sixty Years: The RCAF and CAF Air Command 1924-1984*. Toronto: Canav Books, 1984.

MILBERRY, Larry, and Halliday, Hugh. *The Royal Canadian Air Force at War 1939-1945*. Toronto: Canav Books, 1990.

MOLSON, Kenneth M. *Canada's National Aviation Museum: Its History and Collections*. Ottawa: National Aviation Museum, 1988.

MOLSON, Kenneth M., and Taylor, H. A. *Canadian Aircraft Since 1909*. Stittsville, Ontario: Canada's Wings, 1982.

MOLSON, Kenneth M. *Pioneering in Canadian Air Transport*. [Winnipeg: Jas. A. Richardson], 1974.

ORGAN, R., et al. *Avro Arrow*. Erin, Ontario: Boston Mills Press, 1980.

SUTHERLAND, Alice G. *Canada's Aviation Pioneers: 50 Years of McKee Trophy Winners*. Toronto: McGraw-Hill Ryerson, 1978.

THETFORD, O. G., and Riding, E. J. *Aircraft of the 1914-1918 War*. London: Harleyford, 1954.

THETFORD, Owen. *Aircraft of the Royal Air Force, 1918-1958*. London: Putnam, 1958.

VALDIVIA, Mary H. *At Home in the Sky: The Aviation Art of Frank Wootton*. Washington: Smithsonian Institution Press, 1984.

WHEELER, William J., ed. *The Journal of the Canadian Aviation Historical Society*. Toronto: The Canadian Aviation Historical Society, published quarterly since 1963.

YENNE, Bill. *Lockheed*. Greenwich, Connecticut: Crescent Books, 1987.

YENNE, Bill. *McDonnell Douglas: A Tail of Two Giants*. Greenwich. Connecticut: Crescent Books, 1985.

Credits

Line Illustration Credits

Page	Artist	Title
vi	William Wheeler	Curtiss Lark
viii	Will Davies	Curtiss-Reid Courier
1	Fred H. Varley	Illustration for WWI recruiting poster, CWM
2	Fred H. Varley	Illustrations for WWI recruiting poster, CWM
3	Les Waller	Boeing PT-27
4	Les Waller	D.H. 83 Fox Moth
5	Les Waller	Morane-Saulnier Parasol
6	Les Waller	Vickers Supermarine Walrus
7	Les Waller	Grumman TBM Avenger
8	Les Waller	Vickers Supermarine Spitfire XII
9	Les Waller	Short Sunderland for CAHS
12	Jim Bruce	"Casey" Baldwin and the *Red Wing*
13	George Fuller	Silver Dart silhouette
20	William Wheeler	RFC Nieuport 12
21	William Wheeler	Sopwith Triplane silhouette
36	Tom Bjarnason	Curtiss JN-4 making silent film

Page	Artist	Title
37	William Wheeler	Armstrong Whitworth Siskin silhouette
56	William Wheeler	Stinson SM-1D
57	William Wheeler	Junkers W. 34 silhouette
76	Les Waller	Hawker Typhoons of 198 Squadron, RAF
77	William Wheeler	Hawker Hurricane silhouette
102	Steve Snider	Canadair/Lockheed CF-104s
103	William Wheeler	Canadair/North American F-86 Sabre silhouette
126	Frank Taylor	D.H. 60X Cirrus Moth
128	Frank Taylor	Fairchild KR-34
129	Graham Wragg	Canadair/North American F-86 Sabres
133	Will Davies	Fokker C-II of Fairchild Aerial Surveys
134	Tom Bjarnason	Portrait of the author
135	William Wheeler	Bellanca 66-75 Aircruiser

All illustrations with the exception of those on pages 1, 2, 56, 102 and 135 were prepared for and used in the CAHS *Journal*.

Photographic Credits

Alden Photographic: 35, 47, 61, 65, 75, 81, 83, 87, 95, 99, 105, 107, 113, 115, 117
Aviation Art Canada: 93
Artist's transparency: 39, 85, 91, 119, 121, 123
National Aviation Museum: 17, 23, 25, 27, 29, 33, 41, 49, 51, 55, 59, 69, 71, 111
William Kent: 15, 19, 31, 43, 45, 53, 63, 67, 73, 79, 89, 97, 101, 109
de Havilland Canada: 125

About the Author
William J. Wheeler, BA, AOCA

The author, like so many of the generation who were born in the '30s, has enjoyed a life-long fascination with aviation. He is a native of Port Arthur (now part of Thunder Bay) in Northern Ontario. As a boy, he regularly cycled to the nearby Current River seaplane base, where the Ontario Provincial Air Service operated Norseman and, later, Beaver aircraft. Private operators served the region north of Lake Superior from this base, and many bush planes stopped there on their way west.

He graduated from Port Arthur Collegiate and then attended the Ontario College of Art in Toronto. Upon completing the advertising and design course (for his AOCA), he worked in several Toronto art studios before deciding to freelance as an illustrator. Representing aircraft became a specialty, with assignments from the old Toronto *Star Weekly*, de Havilland Canada, and book publishers such as Macmillan of Canada, Ginn and Company, Clarke Irwin, Longmans Canada, Copp Clark and McClelland and Stewart. At the time, Robert Bradford, then working for Avro Canada,

and later de Havilland Canada, was the only other Toronto illustrator specializing in painting aeroplanes.

Bill Wheeler began teaching high school in the late '60s, and for the past 20 years he has been head of the Art Department at West Hill Collegiate in Scarborough. Along the way he added a BA, mostly in fine art, from the University of Toronto, to his AOCA.

In 1962, he was one of the half-dozen aviation enthusiasts who founded the Canadian Aviation Historical Society, and he has remained a director of the Society ever since.

He was instrumental in launching the Society's *Journal* (as its designer) and, in 1964, he became editor, a function he still performs. Many of the most respected names in Canadian aviation have contributed articles, helping the *Journal* to meet its stated goal of "collecting, preserving and disseminating the history of Canadian aviation." Retaining his contacts in the commercial art field, the author has arranged for *Journal* covers to feature work by artists numbered among Canada's leading illustrators. Several of these paintings are included in this book.

The development of aviation art has been an absorbing interest for Bill Wheeler, dating from boyhood exposure to *Flying Aces* and *Air Trails* magazines, as well as the aviation 'pulps' which are now prized by collectors. As a student of the subject he has become familiar with the work of artists extending back to aviation's infancy. He has spoken about these men and their paintings, the first time at a CAHS Convention in 1973, and has written about Canadian painters of aeroplanes for the *Journal*.

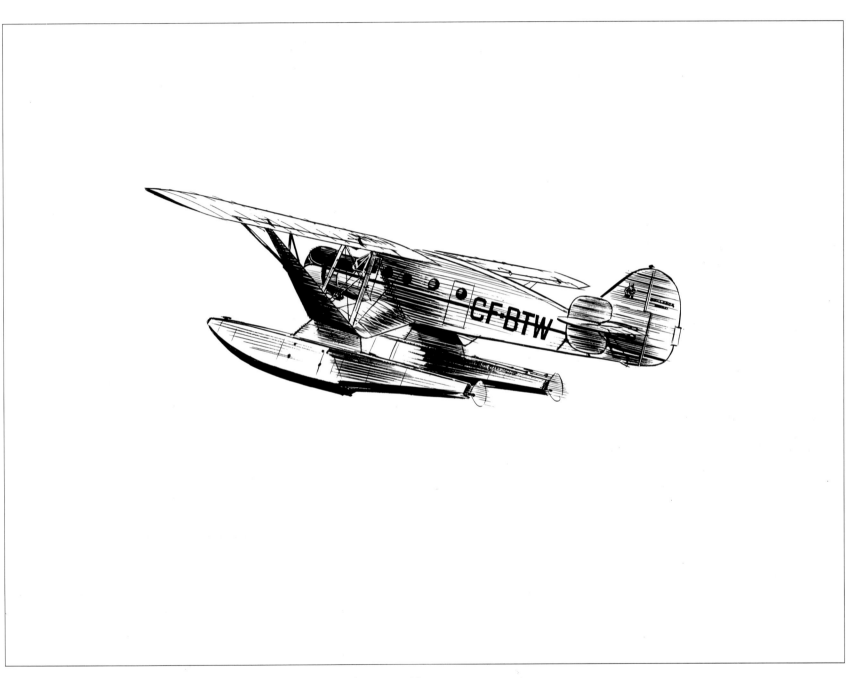

Bellanca 66-75 Aircruiser
William Wheeler